7

THE GOVERNMENT CORPORATION:

ELEMENTS OF A MODEL CHARTER

by Sidney D. Goldberg, LL.B.

and Harold Seidman, Ph.D.

PUBLIC ADMINISTRATION SERVICE

CHICAGO

WASHINGTON   SAN FRANCISCO

338.74
G 618g

FOREWORD

The Government Corporation: Elements of a Model Charter was originally developed in 1947 for the use of staff of the Bureau of the Budget dealing with Government corporations. In view of the frequent requests from both within and outside the Government for information concerning the organization and status of United States Government Corporations, the original memorandum has been substantially revised and brought up to date and is being made available for general use.

While representatives of many Government agencies were consulted in its preparation, responsibility for the views expressed in this paper is solely that of its authors. The suggestions as to language and the brief comments on the law should be regarded primarily as starting points for consideration and research in the light of the special circumstances in each case, since to each of these generalizations there may be appropriate exceptions of greater or lesser importance.

SIDNEY D. GOLDBERG
HAROLD SEIDMAN

CONTENTS

PREFACE

The Government Corporation: Elements of a Model Charter
marks another milestone in the acceptance of the corporation as
a useful instrumentality of the Federal Government. It follows
logically upon the adoption of the Government Corporation Control Act and should be, and I understand already has been, helpful to interested agencies and individuals in the Government.

I have particular interest in these developments because of the
wide use made of corporations during the war by the Office of
Inter-American Affairs, of which I was Coordinator. We utilized
corporations not only for the reasons outlined in this book but
also for two other reasons.

In the first place, the corporations were organized to carry for-
ward action programs in other countries, which meant that our
corporations were guests within those countries and should and
could live within the requirements of the laws of the host countries. This fact alleviated the understandable fear, particularly of
the small countries, of having our Government operating within
their borders.

In the second place, many of our programs were based on the
principle of a three- to five-year contract with the foreign government under which both governments bound themselves to con-
tribute, but the United States' participation declined with each
succeeding year while the other government's participation cor-
respondingly increased. It would have been difficult if not impossible to make such arrangements satisfactorily under annual
appropriations.

During the war years, the rules applicable to Government corporations were ill-defined. The result was a sometimes convenient
and sometimes risky flexibility on the one hand; the concern and,
at times, opposition from such agencies as the General Account-

ing Office and the Bureau of the Budget on the other. The resulting uncertainties and confusion would now seem to be substantially eliminated. I imagine that the risk today may be that the
rules are becoming too rigid. An important quality of the corporation is its adaptability to the needs of different situations. It is
because of this that it has been so widely used to serve all forms
of private groups. If in Government it becomes stereotyped it
will lose a substantial part of its usefulness. I hope that this book
will be regarded as a helpful guide rather than a set of specifications requiring exact conformity.

NELSON A. ROCKEFELLER

PART I. INTRODUCTION

1. Background

The corporation is popularly believed to be a machine-age invention. While vast industrial empires symbolized by such corporations as General Electric and General Motors are peculiarly twentieth century phenomena, the corporation itself is of very ancient lineage. Bodies corporate possessing common treasuries and legal personality separate and distinct from that of the individuals composing them were well known under Roman law. The requirement that corporations obtain a charter or license from the state goes back as far as 205 A.D.

Use of the corporate form of organization for public or quasi-public purposes considerably antedates the modern business corporation. Indeed, early corporations have more in common with present-day Government corporations than their private counterparts. Under the mercantilist political philosophy, corporations were looked upon as arms of the state, performing for the state certain functions of a public character. Even in America, during the nineteenth century, state legislatures rarely were willing to grant corporate privileges, except upon showing that some public purpose would be fulfilled thereby. As a result American corporations were at first largely limited to "internal improvements" —turnpikes, canals, and local utilities. The corporation is obviously not a Johnny-come-lately among Government agencies.

It is true, however, that the Federal Government made little use of the corporate form of organization until comparatively recent times. The United States acquired the Panama Railroad Company in 1904 when it purchased the assets of the French New Panama Canal Company, but it was not until World War I

1

that the first wholly owned Government corporations were created. Of the World War I corporations, only the Federal Land Banks have survived to the present day. With the coming of the depression in the 1930's and the rapid expansion of federal responsibilities for social and economic programs, including many of a business nature, the Government began to utilize increasingly the corporate form of organization. It had become apparent that the traditional government organization did not readily lend itself to the effective administration of business-type operations.

This development was viewed by many with considerable alarm. Senator Schall stated on the floor of the Congress:

> About a year and four months ago President Roosevelt and four Cabinet Generals and nine bureaucracy Colonels crossed over into Delaware, established their camp in Wilmington, and organized six holding corporations with which to make an assault on the Republic of the United States and make of it a United States of Soviet Russia.[1]

In 1944 the Chamber of Commerce of the United States recommended that "no more Government corporations be created [and] that existing corporations be liquidated as soon as possible." The major objection to use of the corporate device, absence of effective executive and congressional control, was eliminated by enactment of the Government Corporation Control Act in 1945.

Government Corporation Control Act

The passage of the Government Corporation Control Act marked the coming of age of the Government corporation in the United States. The act, in effect, represents a recognition by the Congress that the corporation has now become an accepted instrument of government and should not only be accorded the privileges but also should be made to bear the responsibilities of such a status. But while making corporations fully accountable to both the President and the Congress, the act does not attempt to force them into the standard agency mold. New types of controls and procedures are provided, notably the business-type

---

[1] 79 *Cong. Rec.* 4049 (March 20, 1935).

budget and commercial audit, so that those special character-
istics which distinguish a corporation from an agency may be pre-
served. It is highly significant that the Hoover Commission, while
it disagreed strongly about various details of corporate operations,
unquestioningly accepted the corporation as an appropriate instrument for governmental purposes and recommended the incorporation of certain noncorporate federal enterprises such as
the Alaska Railroad and the Washington National Airport.

The Government Corporation Control Act has had important
by-products. Successful experience with the new types of controls provided in the act has led to major reforms in the budget,
accounting, and auditing system of the Government as a whole.
The Bureau of the Budget has extended the business-type budget
to a number of unincorporated business activities. In large meas-
ure the "performance" budget recommended by the Hoover Commission represents a modification of the business-type budget
adapted to the requirements of nonbusiness programs. Emphasis
in governmental accounting has shifted from negative controls
designed primarily to prevent the overobligation of appropriated
funds to modern accounting systems which fully disclose the
financial results of operations. The Budget and Accounting Procedures Act of 1950 stresses the need for maintaining accounting
systems which will furnish adequate financial information for
management purposes and authorizes the gradual elimination of
procedures based on antiquated requirements of law.[1] This act
also authorizes the Comptroller General to change the time and
place of his audit, and he has now instituted the "comprehensive
audit," which combines features of both a government or legality
audit and a commercial-type audit.

Similarities Between Agencies and Corporations

Despite some resemblance to its private prototype in outward
form and operating methods, from the viewpoint of purpose and
over-all Government organization, the Government corporation
is merely another agency of Government. A Government corpora-

---

[1] Walter F. Frese, "Recent Developments in Federal Government Accounting,"
Municipal Finance, November, 1952.

tion cannot be employed as a device to enlarge the constitutional authority of the Federal Government. Establishment of a Government corporation is only justifiable when it is essential for the accomplishment of some public purpose authorized by law. In this respect all Government agencies, corporate and noncorporate, are identical.

Government corporations, unlike private corporations, cannot and should not be wholly autonomous. A Government corporation is an integral part of the federal structure. Corporate programs may be closely related to or affect other governmental programs. The mere fact of corporate existence in no way reduces the need for integration and coordination. As in the case of any other Government agency, the relationship of a corporation to existing departments, the President, and the Congress should be defined in such a way as to focus responsibility, facilitate coordination with related programs, and insure consistency in over-all policy.

The issue of corporate autonomy was brought to a head in 1938 when Arthur E. Morgan, Chairman of the Tennessee Valley Authority, insisted that the TVA was responsible to the Congress rather than to the President and refused to answer questions asked by President Roosevelt. President Roosevelt then handed Mr. Morgan the following memorandum, together with a request for his resignation:

> I must greatly consider the continuing operations of an important Government agency. It would violate my constitutional duty to take care that the laws are faithfully executed if I should leave unsupported charges hanging indefinitely over the heads of two officials who have cooperated in the difficult task of divided authority and thereby permit a recalcitrant, noncooperative official freedom to sabotage Government operations at a crucial time. Finally, I must also consider the consequences of permitting the establishment of a precedent whereby any subordinate in the executive branch of the Government can refuse to give his superior facts sought in order to straighten out difficulties.[1]

---

[1] S. Doc. 155, 75th Cong., 3rd sess., p. 105.

President Roosevelt's removal of Mr. Morgan was upheld by the courts.

Differences Between Agencies and Corporations

While the procedures permitted under the Budget and Accounting Procedures Act of 1950, together with the increased use of revolving funds, have considerably narrowed the gap between agencies and corporations, there continue to be significant differences, mostly at the operating level. It should be noted, however, that the distinguishing attributes of a Government corporation stem not from the fact of incorporation but from the specific grants of power that have been customarily included in the corporate charters enacted by the Congress. With the exception of the Government Corporation Control Act and acts which by reason of their definition of "agencies" as including corporations are applicable, there are no general declarations of congressional policy defining the nature, authority, and immunities of wholly owned Government corporations.

The distinguishing attributes of a Government corporation may be briefly summarized as follows:

1. **Legal Status.** Unlike a normal type Government agency, a body corporate is a separate entity for legal purposes and customarily can sue and be sued, and enter into contracts and acquire property in its own name. Corporations conducting business in their own name have been generally given greater freedom in making contracts and acquiring and disposing of property than ordinary agencies.

2. **Authority to Make Expenditures.** A corporation is usually given power "to determine the character of and the necessity for its expenditures, and the manner in which they shall be incurred, allowed, and paid." A corporation is thus exempted from most of the regulatory and prohibitory statutes applicable to the expenditure of public funds. A corporation's administrative expenses are fixed annually by Congress, but no quantitative limits are placed on its program expenditures as long as such expenditures are made in

accordance with its charter and its annual budget program as approved by Congress.

3. Accounts. The accounting systems of Government corporations normally follow private commercial practice and are designed to reflect all costs properly attributable to the operation, including interest on the Government's investment, depreciation, and the cost of any services furnished to the corporation by other Government agencies. The latter costs would not ordinarily be reflected in the accounts of a noncorporate agency. A corporation is directly responsible for prescribing its own accounting system and keeping its accounts up to date. An agency develops its own accounting system in accordance with standards prescribed by the Comptroller General and subject to his approval.

4. Budget. Corporations present business-type budgets which are essentially plans of operation "with due allowance for flexibility." A corporation seeks congressional approval of its budget program as a whole, unlike an agency which requests specific appropriations. A business-type budget includes such items as a statement of financial condition, a statement of income and expense, a statement of sources and application of funds, and such other supplementary statements and information as are necessary or desirable to make known the financial condition and operations of the corporation. A business-type budget also includes estimates of operations by major types of activities, together with estimates of administrative expenses, borrowings, and any capital funds which are to be returned to the Treasury.[1]

5. Audit. Corporations are audited by the Comptroller General "in accordance with principles and procedures applicable to commercial corporate transactions." A commercial-type audit does not contemplate a review of the legality of each item of expenditure, as does the usual Government audit. The Comptroller General does not ordinarily have authority to disallow corporate transactions. A commercial audit report includes statements of assets and liabilities,

---

[1] See "Appendix" for examples of business-type budget statements.

capital and surplus or deficit, income and expenses, sources and application of funds, together with such other comments and information as the Comptroller General may deem necessary to keep the Congress informed of the operations and financial condition of the corporation. Financial transactions of noncorporate agencies are audited by the General Accounting Office in accordance with such principles and procedures and rules and regulations as may be prescribed by the Comptroller General.

The information which is provided by the business-type budget and the commercial-type audit is not generally available for regular agencies. Without such information, the President and the Congress could not appraise the effectiveness of programs of a business nature or establish adequate controls over them.

6. **Method of Financing.** A very great part of the difference between a corporation and an agency arises from the method of financing its operations. Except for those which have revolving funds, agencies are generally financed by direct annual appropriations from Congress and, in the absence of specific statutory authority, unobligated appropriations may not be carried over from one fiscal year to another. Any revenues which may be derived from agency operations must ordinarily be turned over to the Treasury.

A corporation's funds are generally derived from appropriations to its capital fund, which are not subject to fiscal year limitations, borrowings from the Treasury, and revenues. A corporation is authorized to use and reuse its revenues.

7. **Personnel.** Several corporate charters have recognized the need for greater flexibility in the handling of personnel. Some corporations are exempted from the Civil Service laws and Classification Act, and most of them have been given special powers to employ attorneys and agents.

Significance of Corporate Powers

The special powers granted to corporations are designed to enable the Government, when it undertakes a program predominantly of a business nature, to render service and discharge its obligations to the public as nearly as possible in the same manner as a private business. Flexibility with respect to expenditures, for example, is essential when financial requirements fluctuate with customer demand and consequently cannot be predicted with accuracy. If adequate service is to be provided, the number of passengers to be transported on the Panama Railroad, the volume of freight to be handled by the Inland Waterways Corporation, the amount of paper to be discounted by the Intermediate Credit Banks, and similar operations cannot be made subject to annual expenditure limitations. As in the case of a private corporation, the revenues of a Government corporation increase with the expansion in its business, and the additional expenditures by the corporation to meet increased demand do not ordinarily increase the net expenditures of the U. S. Government. Freedom from restrictive statutes with respect to disbursements, contracts, purchases, and personnel make it possible for a Government corporation, where desirable, to follow standard commercial practices in carrying on its business. In addition, businessmen are familiar with the corporate form of organization and feel more at home in doing business with a corporation than with a Government agency. The businessman knows that a corporation can sue and be sued, but he is not always certain of his rights and obligations with respect to an agency.

Number of Active U. S. Government Corporations

There are at present 37 active wholly owned Government corporations; namely: the Commodity Credit Corporation, Export-Import Bank, Federal Intermediate Credit Banks (12), Production Credit Corporations (12), Federal Crop Insurance Corporation, Federal National Mortgage Association, Federal Prison Industries, Inc., Inland Waterways Corporation, Institute of Inter-American Affairs, Panama Canal Company, Public Housing Administration, Federal Savings and Loan Insurance Corporation, Reconstruction Finance Corporation, Virgin Islands Corporation, and Tennessee Valley Authority. In addition, there are 13 mixed-ownership corporations whose capital stock is owned in part by other than the Federal Government; namely, the Central Bank for Cooperatives, and 12 Banks for Cooperatives. Both the wholly owned and the mixed-ownership corporations operate principally in five major functional fields: (a) aids to industry; (b) aids to housing; (c) aids to agriculture; (d) aids to international relations and trade; and (e) aids to regional and local development. They engage in a wide variety of business-type operations such as making loans and guaranteeing loans of private institutions to businessmen, farmers, home owners, foreign governments, and other borrowers; insuring private individuals against loss from crop failures, price declines, and other hazards; operating power plants, railroads, hotels, steamship and barge lines, terminals, and harbor facilities; distributing electric power; and purchasing, stockpiling, and selling commodities in foreign and domestic markets.

Criteria for Use of Corporations

While the Government corporation has demonstrable advantages over the agency type of organization when it comes to the administration of certain types of programs, it should not be employed indiscriminately. The Government corporation is wholly unsuited to the usual type of agency operation. President Truman laid down the criteria for the use of corporations in his 1948 Budget Message.[1] The use of the corporate form of organization is normally indicated only when a program

1. Is predominantly of a business nature;
2. Is revenue producing and potentially self-sustaining;
3. Involves a large number of business-type transactions with the public;
4. Requires greater flexibility than the customary type of appropriation budget ordinarily permits.

Elements of a Corporation Charter

In the absence of general federal incorporation laws, there has been in the past a wide variance in the powers conferred upon

---

[1] H. Doc. 19, 80th Cong., pp. M57-M62.

different corporations created by the Congress for governmental purposes and in the form, organization, and language of the various charters of such corporations. While absolute uniformity is neither possible nor desirable, for a corporation charter must take into account the program and any peculiar operating or organizational problems of the corporation, a need exists for some standards against which individual corporation charters can be measured. This study was developed as a first step in that direction.

Part II discusses the provisions of a corporation charter under six general heads:

1. **Formal parts,** including the words of corporate creation, its name, legal residence, and the duration of its existence.

2. **General powers,** consisting of an itemization of the basic acts which the corporation is to be permitted to perform, such as making contracts, expending its funds, and using the courts to sue and be sued.

3. **Specific powers,** or a description of the particular activities in which the corporation may engage.

4. **Management,** specifying the persons who are to determine the policies of the corporation and are to control its operations.

5. **Financing,** covering the amount and source of its capital and other funds.

6. **Miscellaneous provisions,** such as payments in lieu of taxes and other grants of authority necessary for or peculiar to the corporation.

PART II. ELEMENTS OF A GOVERNMENT CORPORATION CHARTER

2. Formal Parts

Corporate Creation

Suggested Language

Sec. 1. For the purpose of _____ *there is hereby created, subject to the direction and supervision of the President, or of the head of such agency as he may designate, a body corporate to be known as* _____.

Comment

The establishment of Government agencies, particularly those which deal with the public, has generally been regarded as within the functions of the Congress. Controversies have arisen in the past as to whether adequate authority existed in the executive branch for the creation of certain Government corporations. This problem has been settled by section 304 (a) of the Government Corporation Control Act[1] which provides that no corporation shall be organized or acquired, for the purpose of acting as an agency or instrumentality of the United States, except by Act of Congress or pursuant to specific congressional authority for such action.

This paragraph consists of four distinct parts:

1. The statement of the general objective or function of the corporation, boiled down to a few lines, so that its general purpose will be apparent at first glance.

---

[1] 59 Stat. 597; 31 U.S.C. secs. 841-869. See "Appendix" for a copy of this act.

2. Words creating a body corporate, which are necessary to show clearly that it is a corporation that is being created.

3. The designation of a name so that the corporation can carry on, in its own name, the activities authorized by the charter.

4. A statement of the Chief Executive's responsibility to control the management, either directly or indirectly.

The first three parts of the paragraph appear to require little further comment, items (2) and (3) constituting indispensable elements of corporate existence. The name, however, should ordinarily include one of those words, such as "company," "corporation," or "authority," which are commonly recognized as marks of identification of a corporation.

The organizational location of a Government corporation within the executive branch of the Government should be determined by the same considerations as those applicable to noncorporate agencies. The location of a corporation and its relationship to the President and other departments, agencies, and corporations, as in the case of any governmental activity, should be such as to facilitate coordination with related programs, both corporate and noncorporate, and to insure consistency in over-all Government policy. Sufficient flexibility should be provided to permit adjustments and readjustments in organizational arrangements to meet changing conditions. If the readjustments necessary to meet changed circumstances are not made, and it is impossible to foresee in advance all of the changes which may occur, organization may become a major obstacle rather than an aid to sound management.

The suggested language provides the necessary flexibility. Corporations are made subject to the direction and supervision of the President or the head of such agency as he may designate. In some instances, depending upon the nature and magnitude of the program, the President may choose to have the corporation report directly to him. In others he may designate an appropriate agency head to act for him in exercising general direction over a corporation. The President may make such adjustments in these arrangements as are necessary to meet changed conditions.

If, however, the charter should provide that a corporation be established within a department or agency, it is essential that the corporation be placed under the supervision of the head thereof. Otherwise, the department head could not properly be held accountable to the President and the Congress for securing necessary coordination and consistency in policy.

Succession

Suggested Language

Sec. 2. The corporation shall have succession until June 30, 19___, unless sooner dissolved by Act of Congress.

Comment

The term of existence to be assigned to a proposed corporation depends on the nature of the function to be performed as well as on the estimated completion date of the program. Limited succession is indicated both in the case of emergency or short-term programs and those which are experimental or which may be seriously affected by changing conditions. Perpetual existence has generally been reserved for corporations created to render services which the Government must continue to provide throughout the foreseeable future, for those having certain banking and insurance functions, and for those involved in long-range developmental programs.

Offices, Residence, and Venue

Suggested Language

Sec. 3. The corporation shall have its principal office in the _____ and shall be deemed, for purposes of venue in civil actions, to be a resident thereof. The corporation may establish offices in such other place or places as it may deem necessary or appropriate in the conduct of its business.

Comment

General incorporation laws customarily require the statement, in the charter of each corporation, of the location of its principal place of business. This provision is useful in determining the site of the corporate entity where at least an agent or officer must be available for service of process.[1] It does not determine where the bulk of its business is carried on—which may or may not be at the same place. The term "principal office" is used advisedly, since the Attorney General, in approving the removal from Washington to New York of the bulk of activities of the Federal Savings and Loan Insurance Corporation, noted that the charter[2] fixed the site of "the principal office" in the District of Columbia.[3] He held that as long as the chief administrative officers of the company continued to make their nominal headquarters in Washington, there would be no objection to the transaction of most of its business at a more convenient place. In the event, therefore, that the corporation's principal activities are to be centered at a place other than the District of Columbia, consideration should be given to the establishment of principal offices both at that place and at the seat of Government.

Section 1391(c) of Title 28, United States Code, provides that a corporation may be sued in any of the following places: (a) where it is incorporated, (b) where it is licensed to do business, and (c) where it is actually doing business. The suggested language is in conformity with this section. If it should be appropriate, however, to restrict the venue of actions against the corporation, language for that purpose should be included in this section. This question of venue is more fully discussed under the subhead "jurisdiction" in connection with the "sue and be sued" clause.

---

[1] See Rules of Civil Procedure, sec. 4 (d) (5).
[2] 12 U.S.C., sec. 1725
[3] 40 Op. Atty. Gen., July 26, 1941

3. General Powers

Introductory

Suggested Language

Sec. 4. To carry out the specific powers herein authorized, the corporation shall have the following general powers:

Comment

This section draws a distinction between "general powers," i.e., those which are common to most corporations and which enable them to function, and the "specific powers," which are peculiar to and, in effect, outline the program of the particular corporation.

Seal

Suggested Language

(a) To adopt, alter, and use a corporate seal.

Comment

Virtually all executive departments and agencies of the Federal Government including Government corporations, as well as the United States itself,[1] have and use impression seals. Seals, moreover, are in common use by private corporations. In the case of Government corporations their value lies: (a) in identifying official documents; (b) in the weight given such seals by local law dealing with substantive matters, such as presumption of consideration, and with procedural matters such as the admissibility of records as evidence; (c) in the protection afforded by federal criminal statutes against either forging the official seal[2] or im-

---

[1] 4 U.S.C. sec. 41
[2] 18 U.S.C. sec. 506

properly affixing the true seal to an unauthorized document.[1] The seal adopted pursuant to this authority will be judicially noticed.[2]

By-Laws

Suggested Language

(*b*) *By its board of directors to adopt, amend, and repeal by-laws governing the conduct of its business and the performance of the powers and duties granted to or imposed upon it by law.*

Comment

The authority of a private corporation to enact by-laws, although inherent in the corporate form, is regarded as of so much importance that it is rarely, if ever, left to rest solely in implication. As a general rule, therefore, the power to make by-laws is expressly conferred either in the law or in the charter from which the corporate existence is derived.[3]

In absence of provision to the contrary, however, the authority to make by-laws resides in the stockholders or members of the corporation[4] who may, of course, delegate that power to the board of directors. The validity of corporate by-laws (in this case, regulations), even as a limitation on the ostensible authority of corporate officials to bind the corporation, was sustained in *Federal Crop Insurance Corporation* v. *Merrill et al.*[5]

Property

Suggested Language

(*c*) *To acquire in any lawful manner, any property, real, personal, or mixed, tangible or intangible, or any interest therein; to hold, maintain, use, and operate the same; and to sell, lease, or otherwise dispose of the same at such time, in such manner, and*

---

[1] *Ibid.*, sec. 1017.

[2] See *Keyser* v. *Hitz*, 133 U.S. 138; see also Reviser's Notes, H. Rept. 308, 80th Cong., p. A148, under the heading of Section 1733, on enactment of Title 28, United States Code.

[3] Fletcher, 8 *Cyclopedia of the Law of Private Corporations* (1931 ed.) 643.

[4] *Ibid.*, 645.

[5] 332 U.S. 380.

to the extent deemed necessary or appropriate to carry out the purpose of the corporation.

Comment

The property of wholly owned corporations is regarded, at least equitably, as property of the United States.[1] In the absence, therefore, of authority similar to that conferred by this subsection, such property might be subject to the constitutional provision [2] that only the Congress shall adopt measures for the disposition of federal property, and to all the other safeguards surrounding property whose legal title is in the name of the United States.

This doctrine of beneficial ownership by the United States of corporate property operates to invoke against a thief or wrongdoer all the penalties applicable to crimes against the property of the Government. Moreover, section 6 of Title 18, United States Code, defines "agency" to include Government corporations, and their property, therefore, so far as crimes against it are concerned, has been placed on a parity with other property of the United States. The character of corporate property as property of the Federal Government is clearly assumed in questions regarding its taxability by state and local governments. This subject is discussed below under the subhead, "Payments in Lieu of Taxes." However, property whose legal title is in a Government corporation would appear to be nevertheless subject to special retaining liens such as a warehouseman's lien.[3]

Disposition of corporate property of a purely administrative character, as distinguished from operational, would seem, notwithstanding the authority that would be conferred by the suggested language, to be within the purview of section 203 of the Federal Property Act. The proceeds of such sales would not, however, revert to the Treasury but would, under the suggested language, stand in the place of the property and be paid into the corporation's account.[4]

---

[1] *Inland Waterways Corp.* v. *Young*, 309 U.S. 517, 524; *Clallam County* v. *United States*, 263 U.S. 341; *Grain Corporation* v. *Phillips*, 261 U.S. 106.

[2] U.S. Const. Art. IV, sec. 3.

[3] *United States* v. *Edgerton & Sons, Inc.*, 178 F. 2d 763.

[4] See also section 204 (b) of the Federal Property Act.

The inclusion of this language in the charter is intended to provide both corporate authority and the authority of law required by section 3736 of the Revised Statutes [1] for the purchase of land. Where, however, structures are to be erected on the land, the Attorney General has asserted [2] that the provisions of section 355 of the Revised Statutes [3] are applicable and that his opinion is necessary as to the validity of the title to be acquired.

For the purchase, by a Government corporation, of real property situated within the boundaries of a state, the consent of that state would not be necessary. Unless such consent were obtained, however, the United States would acquire no political or exclusive jurisdiction over it,[4] and would be limited to the rights necessary to discharge the particular function involved. It may be stated, parenthetically, that some Government attorneys feel that most of the problems arising out of conflicts of jurisdiction can be solved more readily under state jurisdiction.

Although it is the well-established policy of the Federal Government to act as self-insurer of its property, the peculiar relationship between the United States and its wholly owned corporations has given rise to a relaxation of this rule with respect to the property in the name of those corporations. Except in connection with insurance against loss of valuables in transit, which is covered by the Losses in Shipment Act [5] specifically including Government corporations, the Comptroller General has approved the purchase of general insurance in the corporate name covering loss of property.[6]

Gifts

Suggested Language

(*d*) *To accept gifts or donations of services, or of property, real, personal or mixed, tangible or intangible, in aid of any of the purposes herein authorized.*

---

[1] 41 U.S.C. sec. 14.
[2] 37 Op. Atty. Gen. 34, 38; 38 Op. Atty. Gen. 31.
[3] 40 U.S.C. sec. 255.
[4] U.S. Const. Art. I, sec. 8; 10 Op. Atty. Gen. 34, 38; 38 Op. Atty. Gen. 31.
[5] 5 U.S.C. secs. 134-134h.
[6] 21 Comp. Gen. 928.

Comment

The United States, as a body politic with the right to acquire and hold property,[1] is authorized, so long as there is no specific statutory prohibition, to accept gifts.[2] It is, however, the settled policy of the Federal Government not to accept, without congressional approval, any gift of property that might require the expenditure of public funds for its care or preservation.[3] The operation of this rule was illustrated in connection with the estate of the late Justice Oliver Wendell Holmes who bequeathed to the United States his Washington residence as well as the residue of his estate. The joint resolution of June 22, 1938 [4] specifically authorized the Attorney General to accept title to the real property, but as to the money, its acceptance was assumed, and provision made for the appointment of a committee to make recommendations to the Congress concerning the use to be made of it.

The departments and officers of the Government are forbidden to accept voluntary services for the Government.[5]

Inasmuch as a corporation, in the course of its operations, may be in a position where it can usefully acquire property or services for a nominal consideration or without payment of any consideration, and can exercise its discretion about assuming obligations with respect to such acquisitions, this power should be included.

Borrowing

Suggested Language

(e) *To borrow from the Treasury of the United States, for any of the purposes of the corporation, sums of money not to exceed a total of _____ outstanding at any time. For this purpose the corporation may issue to the Secretary of the Treasury its notes, debentures, bonds, or other obligations to be redeemable at the option of the corporation before maturity in such manner*

---

[1] 10 Op. Atty. Gen. 34, 38.
[2] *Fay* v. *United States*, 204 Fed. 559.
[3] 30 Op. Atty. Gen. 527.
[4] 52 Stat. 943.
[5] *Rev. Stat.* 3679, 31 U.S.C. sec. 665.

as may be stipulated in such obligations. Each such obligation shall bear interest at a rate determined by the Secretary of the Treasury, taking into consideration the current average rate on outstanding marketable obligations of the United States as of the last day of the month preceding the issuance of the obligations of the corporation. The Secretary of the Treasury is authorized and directed to purchase any obligations of the corporation to be issued hereunder and for such purpose the Secretary of the Treasury is authorized to use as a public-debt transaction the proceeds from the sale of any securities issued under the Second Liberty Bond Act, as amended, and the purposes for which securities may be issued under the Second Liberty Bond Act, as amended, are extended to include any purchases of the corporation's obligations hereunder.

Comment

It was formerly the common practice to authorize Government corporations to issue their own obligations to the public with principal and interest guaranteed by the Federal Government. The President, however, in his 1948 Budget Message,[1] recommended that the authority of Government corporations to issue guaranteed obligations to the public be repealed and that they be limited in the future to borrowing funds solely from the Treasury. This message also recommended that corporations be required to reimburse the Treasury for the cost of the money advanced to them.

It is believed that centralized financing by the Treasury avoids competition in the investment market between the Treasury and other Government agencies and makes for fiscal efficiency and economy. This is considered especially important at the present time because of the magnitude and complexity of the problems involved in the management of the public debt.

In those few remaining instances where authority still exists for issuance of debentures to the public, the Secretary of the Treasury, under section 303 (a) of the Government Corporation

---

[1] H. Doc. 19, 80th Cong., p. M58.

Control Act,[1] must approve any issue as to form, timing, maturity, and price.

The direction to the Secretary of the Treasury to treat loans to corporations as a "public debt transaction" permits him to use any funds in his possession rather than restrict him to funds appropriated to him for such purpose. Other forms of financing are considered preferable to borrowing from public debt receipts. This method of financing is now largely restricted to emergency programs. For preferred method of financing, see pages 56-9.

Contracts

Suggested Language

(f) *To enter into and perform such contracts, leases, cooperative agreements, or other transactions as may be necessary in the conduct of its business and on such terms as it may deem appropriate, with any agency or instrumentality of the United States, or with any state, territory or possession, or with any political subdivision thereof, or with any person, firm, association, or corporation.*

Comment

Without power to enter into contracts on terms that might not necessarily be within the authority of ordinary agencies of the Government, the usefulness of a corporation would be seriously impaired. The suggested language is fairly broad and would permit a wide range of contracts. Some of the limitations, however, imposed by statute on the contracts of the Government, including Government corporations, should be noted.

In any contract for materials or supplies in an amount exceeding $10,000 there must be included the provisions of the Walsh-Healey Act [2] making the production of such materials or supplies subject to regulation with respect to minimum wages, maximum hours of labor, prohibition of child labor, and safety of working conditions.

---

[1] 31 U.S.C. sec. 868a.
[2] Act of June 30, 1936, 41 U.S.C. secs. 35-45.

Purchases of goods and materials for the use of the Government of the United States must be from American producers or manufacturers.[1] This requirement prevails in all cases unless there be an affirmative legal declaration that procurement of American-produced or American-manufactured materials would be inconsistent with the public interest.

The requirement of section 3741 of the Revised Statutes[2] that every contract shall include an express condition that no member of, or delegate to, Congress shall be admitted to any share or benefit therefrom, and the prohibitions in 18 U.S.C. secs. 431 and 432 have posed difficulties in the past with respect to the activities of the Government in fields where Congressmen, not as members of the federal legislature but as private individuals, might have a proper place. Section 433 of Title 18, United States Code, recognizes the fields of agriculture and finance as exceptions, and relaxes the prohibition with respect to them. The field of activity of a Government corporation should be examined, therefore, to determine whether similar relaxation of this safeguard would be appropriate.

In all contracts to be made by Government corporations involving the expenditure of money for *administrative* (as distinguished from operating) transactions the provisions of section 3709 of the Revised Statutes, as revised by the act of August 2, 1946[3] and section 303 of the Federal Property and Administrative Services Act of 1949,[4] as amended, would govern.

The provisions of the act of June 30, 1932,[5] concerning the maximum rent payable, might not, under the language suggested, be applicable since authority to determine the conditions of the contracts would be conferred.

Contracts involving the purchase or sale of property, and its insurance against loss or damage, are discussed in connection with the subsection authorizing the acquisition and disposition of property.

---

[1] Act of March 3, 1933, 41 U.S.C. sec. 10a.
[2] 41 U.S.C. sec. 22.
[3] *Ibid.*, sec. 5.
[4] 63 Stat. 377.
[5] 40 U.S.C. sec. 278a.

Employees, Attorneys, and Agents

Suggested Language

(g) *To appoint such officers, attorneys, agents, and employees; to vest them with such powers and duties; to fix and pay such compensation to them for their services as the corporation may determine; to require bonds for the faithful performance of their duties, and to pay the premiums therefor.*

Comment

Status. Employees of Government corporations, in the absence of specific statutory provision to the contrary in any given situation, would be considered as employees of the United States.[1] Section 6 of Title 18 and section 451 of Title 28 of the United States Code both define "agency" of the United States as including, for the purposes of those titles, Government corporations. These definitions mark the progress of the general evolution of thinking on this subject, notwithstanding the decisions in *United States* v. *Strang* (254 U.S. 491) and *Pierce* v. *United States* (314 U.S. 306) [2] which, as they involved the enforcement of criminal statutes, understandably called for the strictest possible construction of the then prevailing rule. That some statutes and executive orders of the past two decades include these corporations expressly while others do not is apparently due to the changes of style in legislative language designed to cover the entire executive branch of the Government. Not until 1932 did Government corporations become an important consideration in general legislation, and references in earlier enactments to "departments and independent agencies," to "departments, agencies or independent establishments" and to other combinations of these words have been held, in most cases, to include the wholly

---

[1] 34 Op. Atty. Gen. 363; 23 Comp. Gen. 815.

[2] Holding (prior to the amendment of the impersonation statute to include Government corporation employees) that impersonation of a Government corporation employee was not indictable under the statute respecting impersonation of an employee of the United States.

owned corporations.[1] Employees of Government corporations, moreover, are bracketed with employees of the United States as being not covered in the Labor Management Relations Act.[2]

Scope of Authority. Unlike the agents and employees of private corporations, whose apparent authority, notwithstanding actual limitations, would serve to bind the corporation,[3] the agents and employees of a Government corporation cannot bind the corporations except within the limits of their actual authority, however broad that authority may appear.[4] Moreover, the fact that certain functions of a Government corporation have previously been discharged in a certain manner would not preclude the corporation from changing its methods,[5] although in the case of a private corporation, where a member of the public had changed his position in reliance upon a particular course of conducting business, an estoppel might arise.

However, in cases where the Government corporation was actually authorized to make contracts of various types, but the corporation's clerical employees prepared the wrong type of contract, the courts have applied to this situation the same rule of law that would be applicable between private persons. The Government corporation, therefore, in absence of proof of mutual mistake of fact (rather than a mere clerical error on its part) would have no right to a judicial reformation of the contract.[6]

Compensation. The Classification Act of 1949 [7] is specifically applicable to Government corporations. Title II contains a large number of exemptions covering such corporations as TVA, Inland Waterways Corporation, Virgin Islands Corporation, Panama Canal Company, Federal Intermediate Credit Banks, and such business enterprises as the Alaska Railroad. If a corporation's

[1] *Emergency Fleet Corporation* v. *Western Union Telegraph Company,* 275 U.S. 415; 37 Op. Atty. Gen. 437; 27 Comp. Gen. 140; 26 Comp. Gen. 701; 15 Comp. Gen. 485.

[2] P.L. 101, 80th Cong., sec. 101; 29 U.S.C. sec. 152.2.

[3] Fletcher, *Cyclopedia of the Law of Private Corporations,* ch. 11, sec. 453.

[4] *Federal Crop Insurance Corporation* v. *Merrill,* 332 U.S. 380; *Reconstruction Finance Corporation* v. *Martin Dennis,* 3 Cir., 195 F. 2d 698.

[5] *United States ex rel. Tennessee Valley Authority* v. *Moody,* 86 F. Supp. 694.

[6] *Reconstruction Finance Corporation* v. *Childress,* 186 F. 2d 698; *Reconstruction Finance Corporation* v. *Zuvekas,* 196 F. 2d 236.

[7] P.L. 429, 81st Cong.

employees are not to be brought under the Classification Act, a specific exemption such as those given to the agencies listed above is required.

Other statutes bearing upon compensation, however, have been also extended to corporation employees. By the acts approved March 14, 1936 [1] corporation employees, with the exception of those of the Panama Railroad and the farm credit corporations, were placed on an equality with other federal employees with respect to (1) the establishment of a specific work week; [2] (2) the credit of annual leave; [3] and (3) the accrual of sick leave, [4] with permission to the head of the agency to advance not more than 30 days of sick leave if needed. [5] Titles II and III of the Pay Act of 1945 are applicable to them and, accordingly, they are entitled to overtime pay [6] (5 U.S.C. sec. 911, 912) and to differential payments for night or holiday work [7] if earned. For "within-grade" salary increases, credit must be given for service with any corporation. [8] The dual compensation statutes are considered applicable to corporation employees. [9]

For the past few years, each Independent Offices Appropriation Act has contained a provision, applicable to all appropriation acts for that year, forbidding the payment of compensation to any federal employee on duty within the continental United States who is not either a citizen or national of the United States, or who, not being a citizen or a national, has not filed a declaration of intention to become a citizen.

Civil Service. By Executive Order 7916 of June 24, 1938, the President brought into the competitive civil service, "all positions in the Executive civil service, including positions in corporations wholly owned or controlled by the United States," with the ex-

---

[1] 49 Stat. 1161 and 1162; 5 U.S.C. sec. 30j.
[2] 5 U.S.C. sec. 29a; subsequently fixed by the Federal Employees Pay Act of 1945, 5 U.S.C. sec. 944, at 40 hours.
[3] 5 U.S.C. sec. 30b-30e.
[4] *Ibid.,* sec. 30f.
[5] *Ibid.,* sec. 30h.
[6] *Ibid.,* sec. 911, 912.
[7] *Ibid.,* sec. 921, 922.
[8] Executive Order 8882, September 3, 1941.
[9] 23 Comp. Gen. 815.

ception of policy-making positions and positions theretofore or thereafter specifically exempted by the President (Schedule A). Subsequently, under the authority of section 1 of the Ramspeck Act[1] the President issued Executive Order 8743 of April 23, 1941, which covered into the competitive service all officers and employees not theretofore included. Although Executive Order 9830 of February 24, 1947 superseded and by its terms revoked Executive Order 7916, the provision covering the employees of Government corporations may properly be regarded as having been executed and, therefore, unaffected by the revocation. Section 1.1 of the current Civil Service Rules, promulgated by Executive Order 9830, provides that "the competitive service shall include all civilian positions in the executive branch of the Government unless specifically excepted therefrom," and that "whenever there is a doubt the Civil Service Commission shall determine whether a position is in the competitive service." Under this authority the prior view of the Commission, i.e., that all positions are covered, other than those specifically excepted by statute or executive order, was confirmed.

However, it is possible that the activities of the corporation proposed to be authorized may, under some circumstances, justify the exemption of its employees from the Civil Service laws and Classification Act provided, of course, that the system proposed as an alternative is also based upon the merit principle. Section 3 of the Tennessee Valley Authority Act,[2] for example, provides that the authority should

> . . . without regard to the provisions of Civil Service laws applicable to officers and employees of the United States, appoint such . . . employees . . . as are necessary. . . .

If, on the other hand, considerations should justify the exemption of only a few policy-making employees, leaving the bulk of them under the competitive civil service, recourse may be had to the inclusion of these few under Schedule A.

Injuries. The United States Employees' Compensation Act,[3]

---

[1] 5 U.S.C. sec. 631a.
[2] 16 U.S.C. sec. 831b.
[3] 5 U.S.C. secs. 751-801.

although its coverage is expressed [1] merely as over "all civil employees of the United States," may be regarded as covering the employees of Government corporations.[2] As early as 1924 the Attorney General held that employees of the Emergency Fleet Corporation were employees of the United States and entitled to compensation for injuries.[3] The holding in *United States* v. *Strang* [4] was considered but, in view of the proviso in the Urgent Deficiencies Appropriation Act of December 24, 1919,[5] precluding double compensation in the case of Fleet Corporation employees, it was held that the Congress intended that corporation employees should be covered.[6]

In a letter dated March 10, 1945, Chairman Swofford of the Employees' Compensation Commission wrote:

Under the policies of the Commission, the benefits of the Compensation laws have been extended to all persons employed by corporate agencies of the United States.

The Comptroller General has stated that the:

. . . determination of who are entitled to the benefits of the Employees' Compensation Act primarily is a matter for the Employees' Compensation Commission and its determinations in that regard are not, ordinarily, subject to review by the General Accounting Office.[7]

Retirement. In the decade following enactment of the first retirement statute [8] decisions as to its applicability to employees of federal corporations were uniformly in the negative, based upon the opinion in *United States* v. *Strang* (supra). In 1932, however, Attorney General Mitchell held [9] that employees of these corporations were entitled to transfer to the competitive

---

[1] *Ibid.*, sec. 790.
[2] See *Panama Railroad* v. *Minnix*, 282 Fed. 47; *Posey* v. *Tennessee Valley Authority*, 93 F. 2d 726.
[3] 34 Op. Atty. Gen. 120; 34 Op. Atty. Gen. 363.
[4] 254 U.S. 491.
[5] 41 Stat. 377, 5 U.S.C. sec. 795.
[6] See 59 *Cong. Rec.* 854.
[7] Letter to the Director of the Budget, March 26, 1945, B-48553.
[8] Act of May 22, 1920, 41 Stat. 614.
[9] 37 Op. Atty. Gen. 7, 14.

civil service in other agencies of the Government and, in 1936, the Civil Service Commission determined to credit, toward retirement, service rendered in corporations either created by federal statutes requiring majority ownership of their stock by the United States, or in which the officers and directors were appointed in the same manner as federal officials.[1] Direct coverage of employees, that is, the privilege of retirement, was at first confined to those to whom competitive civil service status had been extended and the question of general coverage was not settled until, in view of the specific definition of "department" as including corporations in section 1 of the act of January 24, 1942,[2] the commission definitely held corporation employees, unless subject to another retirement system, to be fully covered under the retirement statutes[3] and directed that payroll deductions be made as in the case of other Government agencies.

Official Bonds. While the responsibility of the officials of a corporation for the prudent management of its affairs would give them implied authority to require employees to post bonds, attention is directed to the expression in Title 6, United States Code, section 14, that:

> The United States shall not pay any part of the premium or other cost of furnishing a bond required by law or otherwise of any officer or employee of the United States.

Accordingly, if it is not deemed desirable to require payment of the premium by the employee, the charter should include express authority for such payment out of corporate funds.

Attorneys. The inclusion of attorneys among the persons whom the corporation is authorized to employ appears to be necessary if the management is to be permitted to determine the amount and kind of legal services needed, to choose the attorneys it believes competent for that purpose, and to have control of its litigation. In the absence of a provision of this kind, the corporation might be considered bound by the requirement of sections

---

[1] Minutes of the Civil Service Commission for May 13, 1936.
[2] 56 Stat. 13.
[3] 5 U.S.C. ch. 14.

189 and 361 of the Revised Statutes [1] that legal services must be obtained from the Attorney General.

Expenditures

Suggested Language

(*h*) *To determine the character of and the necessity for its obligations and expenditures, and the manner in which they shall be incurred, allowed, and paid, subject to provisions of law specifically applicable to Government corporations.*

Comment

The authority granted by this provision is the single most important source of corporate flexibility. It is designed to free the corporation from the necessity of complying with most of the prohibitory and regulatory statutes surrounding the expenditure of appropriated funds, except those specifically applicable to Government corporations.

In discussing language such as that suggested above but which omitted, however, the final clause reading "subject to provisions of law specifically applicable to Government corporations," the Comptroller General has stated: [2]

In the matter of expenditures there is not a clear line of distinction [between corporate-type and departmental-type operations] for the reason that, while corporations were formed largely for the reason that administrators preferred to find a method of procedure which would permit expenditures by whatever rules they, themselves, chose to adopt, this feature has not until very recent times been the subject of general Congressional enactment, and it cannot be said with confidence that Congress has announced a policy with respect to expenditures of corporations as such. Instead, the approach has been to grant to certain corporations an all-inclusive authority to determine for themselves the character and necessity of their expenditures and the manner in which they shall be incurred, allowed, and paid. Where such language

---

[1] 5 U.S.C. secs. 449 and 306.
[2] Letter of December 5, 1947, H. Rept. 1845, 80th Cong., p. 777, Appendix E.

appears in the act chartering the corporation, there can be no question but that Congress has determined that the Congressional or statutory rules otherwise directing how the public monies shall be spent are not of their own force to apply to the corporation, but rather that the corporation shall determine for itself what methods, procedures, etc., should be employed.

The foregoing remarks, however, dealt with an expenditure clause which did not contain the words respecting laws "applicable to Government corporations," and their full import would not be applicable to the language here suggested. While a broad range of freedom remains for corporate selection of the fiscal methods, procedures, and expenditures best indicated to carry out its charter program, there would be required to be followed any statutes specifying their applicability to Government corporations, and any others whose language as a matter of law clearly includes them. Thus, among others, the following, unless specifically excepted, would apply (at least in the case of wholly owned corporations):

1. The Federal Corrupt Practices Act [1] which makes it unlawful for "any corporation organized by authority of any law of Congress, to make a contribution in connection with any election. . . ." While not directed specifically at Government corporations, they would as corporations fall squarely within its terms.

2. The Government Losses in Shipment Act [2] which precludes the payment of premiums for insurance against loss of valuables in shipment, except in accordance with its provisions.

3. The Walsh-Healey Act [3] which requires that, in any contract for the purchase of materials or supplies exceeding $10,000, certain provisions respecting hours and conditions of labor shall be included.

4. Title 18, U. S. Code, section 4124, which provides that federal departments and agencies (including wholly

[1] 2 U.S.C. sec. 251.
[2] 5 U.S.C. sec. 134c.
[3] 41 U.S.C. secs. 35-45.

owned corporations) shall purchase such products of Federal Prison Industries, Inc. as meet their requirements and may be available.

5. Some of the provisions of the Administrative Expense Act,[1] by the definitions contained in section 18 thereof,[2] are specifically made applicable to the transactions of wholly owned Government corporations.

6. The Miller Act[3] which requires that, in connection with any contract over $2,000 for the construction or repair of any public building or public work, there shall be posted (1) a performance bond and (2) a payment bond of 50 per cent of the amount of the contract to assure payment of labor and suppliers of material.

7. The act of July 11, 1947[4] providing for the handling and payment of "stale" checks drawn on the Treasurer of the United States.

8. The Federal Property and Administrative Services Act of 1949.

All of the foregoing must be considered in the light of the essential differences in the methods of accounting and auditing provided for the corporations by the Government Corporation Control Act as compared with those in force for the departments under the Budget and Accounting Act and related laws. This difference was explained at length by the Comptroller General in the letter of December 5, 1947, cited on page 29 above, as follows:

3. *Accounting.*—The matter of accounting is somewhat more readily describable. The accounting required of the department spending the appropriations antedates the formation of our Government. In essence the procedure consists of "advancing" a sum appropriated to an individual officer operating with or for the department responsible for the expenditure. That officer at that time becomes, technically, indebted to the United States for that amount until he "accounts" for the same. This is done by the

---

[1] 60 Stat. 806.
[2] 5 U.S.C. sec. 73b-4.
[3] 40 U.S.C. sec. 270a.
[4] 31 U.S.C. secs. 132-4.

process of showing a lawful expenditure of the sum, with the result that if, in the opinion of the auditors (or, on appeal, of the Comptroller General), the expenditure is shown to have been an unlawful one, no credit is allowed for the item, the officer's indebtedness remains, and he is subject to suit therefor in the United States courts, at which stage the question of legality of the expenditure is tested judicially. The ruling of the accounting officer is binding upon the departments but, of course, is not binding in any way upon Congress or the courts.

In recent years that procedure has been altered slightly for the civilian operations of the Government by the enactment of the Certifying Officers Act, under which the particular person responsible and accountable for the legality of the expenditure is not the fiscal officer to whom the money was advanced and who drew the check, but, rather, is the "certifying officer" who approved the payment on whose approval the disbursing officer relied.

The result, of course, of that audit and settlement procedure is that the payments are made by the administrative officer at the risk of the subsequent disallowance by the General Accounting Officer, and in the event of such disallowance, assuming its correctness, the amount is recoverable by the Government either from the payee who received it in error, or from the officer responsible for the payment, or from his surety. The audit procedure varies widely according to the circumstances and needs of the situation; that is, it may call for a voucher audit here in Washington (which may be more or less detailed), or it may be found more appropriate to make a field audit at the site of the operations. Also, the audit does not necessarily call for a review of each item of expenditure; it is essential that under that plan all expenditures are at least subject to such audit.[1]

On the other hand, the accounting required of corporations proceeds upon a somewhat different basis. In the Government corporation control acts of 1945 Congress directed for the first time that the General Accounting Office undertake annually to make a commercial, corporate type of audit of the financial transactions

---

[1] Revision of these procedures is now under study by the General Accounting Office, the Treasury Department, and the Bureau of the Budget.

of all the Government corporations. Also, the Comptroller General was authorized to utilize that type of audit (in those few cases where the corporations are financed by departmental-type appropriations) for the purpose of settling the accounts of the officers to whom appropriations are advanced. A regulation has just been adopted to that effect, so that the same audit procedure will apply to corporations, whether they be financed by a capital grant or by an annual expenditure type of appropriation. The commercial, corporate type of audit comprehends an examination of the actual books and records of the agency, and a survey of its transactions on a test-check basis, leading up to a comprehensive annual report to the Congress, to the President, and to the corporation. The result, of course, is an over-all or agency-wide survey type of audit which does not necessarily call for examination of detail transactions, but which does include a resume of the entire function under review, its background, authority, and methods of operation.

The remaining significant difference is that the survey type of audit depends upon corrective action being taken by the management or by Congress to prevent future errors, but it does not include any independent machinery for collection back where erroneous payments are found to have been made. On the other hand, the accounting required for appropriations does not call for a survey or periodic report on the operations as a whole, but it does include the element of control of expenditures through the power of disallowance and the specific authority for, and mechanics of, collection back where erroneous disbursements are shown to have occurred.

Sue and Be Sued

Suggested Language

(i) *To sue and be sued in its corporate name.*

Comment

General. The United States, as a body politic, although a government of delegated powers, is nevertheless a sovereign in its own right [1] and enjoys, therefore, the traditional immunity of the

---

[1] *Ruppert* v. *Caffey*, 251 U.S. 264.

sovereign from being sued without its consent. As to Government corporations, however, the relaxation of this sovereign immunity and the grant of authority to bring and defend suits in its own name have been considered major contributions toward the flexibility of operation that makes the corporate form useful, and, in most cases, the right to sue and be sued is contained in the statute or other document creating the corporation. While the Tucker Act of 1887, granting the consent of the United States to be sued in claims on contract, and the Tort Claims Act of 1946, making the United States amenable to suit for certain torts, have greatly reduced the field of sovereign immunity, the authorization that a corporation may "sue and be sued" is still broader than that of the Federal Government and is much less encumbered with procedural and other limitations. Moreover, the right to sue and be sued, coupled with the right to employ attorneys, serves to maintain for the corporation control over its litigation.

The question of whether, in the absence of such authority, the corporation would be suable was discussed by the Supreme Court in *Keifer & Keifer* v. *Reconstruction Finance Corporation and Regional Agricultural Credit Corporation*.[1] The defendant Regional Agricultural Credit Corporation had been created by the defendant Reconstruction Finance Corporation pursuant to the authority contained in section 201 (e) of the Emergency Relief and Construction Act of 1932.[2] In the charter of the agricultural corporation, however, there was no explicit authority to sue and be sued and the question thereupon arose as to whether a suit could be maintained against it. Mr. Justice Frankfurter, for the court, stated that, inasmuch as Congress had uniformly included amenability to suit in all the Government corporations theretofore chartered, an attitude on the part of Congress was thereby revealed that Government corporations in general, including, of course, this corporation, should also be subject to suit. The court also referred to, but did not place its principal reliance upon, another argument which would seem adequate to justify its decision: that is, that inasmuch as the Reconstruction Finance Cor-

[1] 306 U.S. 381.
[2] 47 Stat. 713, 12 U.S.C. sec. 1148.

poration was itself subject to suit it could not pass on to its creature, the agricultural corporation, a sovereign immunity that it did not possess. Whether, in the light of this reasoning, a corporation created by direct congressional charter and omitting the "sue and be sued" clause would nevertheless be subject to suit is a matter for future judicial determination.

The decision in this case is interesting reading in that the court appears to have approached the problem by regarding the Government corporation as an entity which, although created by the Government for Government purposes, stands separate and apart from the federal organization. So viewed, there is validity to the question posed by the court in this case.

"Congress may, of course [it wrote], endow a governmental corporation with the Government's immunity. But always the question is: has it done so?" There is, however, another angle of approach—vaguely defined in this case but clearly stated and utilized by Mr. Justice Brandeis, for the court, in *Emergency Fleet Corporation* v. *Western Union Telegraph Co.*[1] This approach recognizes the Government corporation as an integral part of the United States Government rather than simply as a creation of the Government.

> The Fleet Corporation [he wrote] is entitled to the government rate, not because it is an instrumentality of the Government, but because it is a department of the United States within the meaning of the Post Roads Act.

It is important to point out that the inclusion of the "sue and be sued" clause in a corporate charter merely removes the procedural bar to the commencement of suit that is interposed by the sovereign nature of this arm of the Government. No new causes of action are or could be created by this clause and liability would not be imposed in a case where liability would not otherwise exist. Moreover, there is always the possibility that the Congress may, by legislative enactment, destroy a right of action or regulate the manner of its enforcement, subject, of

[1] 275 U.S. 404.

course, to the constitutional limitation on taking of property without compensation.[1]

Since the Federal Government is a government of delegated powers, each of its activities must be specifically justified in the light of one of the powers of government so delegated. The distinction made in the municipal field generally between activities of a "proprietary" nature and those classified as "governmental," therefore, is not applicable to the Federal Government and its corporations.[2]

There is, however, another type of distinction that properly can be drawn in connection with Government corporations. This one cannot be based, as can the "proprietary-governmental" distinction, principally upon an examination of the character of the specific activities involved, but must be based upon the broad question of public policy as to whether the submission of the particular activity to judicial control would be an encroachment by the judiciary on the functions of either the legislative or the executive branches of the Government. For example, it has been held that the Tennessee Valley Authority, although suable, is not liable for property damage which is primarily attributable to the operation of the program or basic governmental functions for which the authority was established, i.e., flood control and navigation.[3]

In *Adams* v. *Home Owners' Loan Corporation*[4] the corporation was sued for malicious prosecution based upon the acts of its employees in recommending criminal action against the plaintiff. With the collapse of the criminal prosecution, upon the facts involved, the plaintiff might have had a good cause of action against a private corporation. Against the Government corporation, however, the Circuit Court of Appeals held that the duty of the Home Owners' Loan Corporation was to safeguard the

---

[1] See *Monolith* v. *Reconstruction Finance Corporation*, 178 F. 2d 854; certiorari denied, 339 U.S. 932; *Pergament* v. *Frazer*, 93 F. Supp. 9.

[2] *Federal Land Bank of St. Paul* v. *Bismarck Lumber Co. et al.*, 314 U.S. 95, 102.

[3] *Lynn* v. *United States*, 110 F. 2d. 586; *Grant* v. *Tennessee Valley Authority*, 49 F. Supp. 564; *Atchley* v. *Tennessee Valley Authority*, 69 F. Supp. 952 (and see cases there collected); *Malone* v. *Tennessee Valley Authority*, 86 F. Supp. 961.

[4] 107 F. 2d 139.

property of the Government; that in doing so it acted as and for the Government and that the clause of its charter authorizing suits against it would not serve to create a cause of action. In *Pennell* v. *Home Owners' Loan Corporation*,[1] the district court referred to the same principle as a valid test, although rejecting its application in that case.

One particular type of law suit, however, which a Government corporation may neither bring nor be called upon to defend, is one by or against a federal agency or another Government corporation. In *Defense Supplies Corp.* v. *U.S. Lines Co. et al.*,[2] the Circuit Court of Appeals for the Second Circuit affirmed the dismissal of suit in admiralty brought by the libelant, a subsidiary of the Reconstruction Finance Corporation, against the steamship company and the United States, which, through the War Shipping Administration, had chartered the vessel aboard which libelant's shipment had been damaged. The court held that plaintiff and defendant were both in law constituent parts of the Federal Government, and that there did not exist, therefore, the diversity of interest between the parties necessary to the maintenance of the suit. Notwithstanding the unavailability of judicial redress where one corporation has suffered property damage at the fault of another, the Comptroller General has agreed that the funds of a Government corporation (in this case the Inland Waterways Corporation) are available for property damage claims generally, and the corporation would be authorized to pay such a claim to another Government corporation in a proper case.[3]

Jurisdiction. The creation of Government corporations by act of Congress makes suits by or against them "suits of a civil nature arising under the Constitution or laws of the United States." [4] Where, therefore, an action is commenced by a wholly owned

---

[1] 21 F. Supp. 497

[2] 148 F 2d 311, certiorari denied, 326 U.S. 746.

[3] 26 Comp. Gen. 235. For a contrary result in the case of a Government department as the agency at fault, see 25 Comp. Gen. 49, denying the use of Navy Department appropriations to pay claims for damages caused to the property of certain Government corporations.

[4] *Osborn* v. *Bank of the United States*, 9 Wheat. 738.

Government corporation, or if brought against it and the matter in controversy exceeds $3,000 in value, the suit would be within the jurisdiction of the United States district courts.[1] However, since a federally chartered corporation would be considered a domestic, rather than a foreign, corporation in any state where it carries on its activities,[2] there is to be considered the possibility that suit might be commenced in a state court and, although transferable to the federal court, it would be removed, not to the district court in which such suit could have been originally commenced but, under Title 28, United States Code, section 1441, to the district court of the United States for the district in which the state court suit is pending.[3]

In the event, therefore, that the program of the corporation is such that, for reasons of public policy or expediency, it would be better to waive in advance the right to remove and to permit suits against it in any otherwise suitable courts, there might be added to the suggested language the phrase "in any court of competent jurisdiction, federal, state or local."

While clerks in the United States courts have in the past required, in the absence of statutory exemption in the corporate charter, the deposit of advance fees in the same manner as would have been required of any private litigant,[4] Title 28, United States Code, sections 2408 and 2412 (a) appear to have changed this rule. Whether the enactment of these sections also renders the decision in *Reconstruction Finance Corporation* v. *Menihan* [5] obsolete has not yet been judicially determined.[6]

Preliminary Relief. The courts have generally construed the "sue and be sued" clause as placing Government corporations in the same position as private corporations in their standing before

---

[1] Title 28, U.S.C. secs. 1331, 1345; *Federal Intermediate Credit Bank* v. *Mitchell*, 277 U.S. 213; *Sabin* v. *Home Owners' Loan Corporation*, 147 F. 2d 653; *Reconstruction Finance Corporation* v. *Bell*, 84 F. 2d 136.

[2] *Leggett* v. *Land Bank of Columbia*, S.C., 167 S.E. 557; *Jacobsen* v. *Emergency Fleet Corporation*, 217 N.Y. Supp. 856.

[3] *General Investment Company* v. *Lake Shore Ry.*, 260 U.S. 261; *Hill* v. *Emergency Fleet Corporation*, 284 F. 398.

[4] *In re Clerk's Fees*, 49 F. Supp. 1011.

[5] 312 U.S. 81.

[6] See Costs, *infra.*

the courts. One decision, however, along these lines, which has been used as the basis for speculation on the scope of preliminary relief does *not* appear entirely to justify the conclusions which have been drawn from it.[1] In *Federal Land Bank* v. *Priddy*,[2] the Federal Land Bank had applied for and been denied a writ of prohibition to compel a state court to vacate an attachment against it as a foreign corporation. The Supreme Court held that the operation of the "sue and be sued" clause would ordinarily include the right to an attachment before suit and that this remedy would embrace the bank. In its opinion, the court pointed out that the bank involved, although created by the United States, was not intended to be wholly owned by the Government, and that

> . . . They [the land banks] thus have many of the characteristics of private business corporations, distinguishing them from the Government itself . . . and from corporations wholly government owned and created to effect an exclusively governmental purpose.[3]

It is doubtful that this decision justifies a conclusion that extraordinary remedies, such as injunction or mandamus, would be granted against corporations created and wholly owned by the Federal Government. It is well settled that, in the main, the performance by executive officers of duties assigned to them by statute is not subject to judicial restraint.[4] This doctrine does not depend upon the immunity of the Federal Government from unconsented suit but is based upon public policy and the separation of the powers of Government.

While a mandamus or injunction of broad effect, designed to obstruct or suspend one or more of the general functions of a Government corporation, would probably not be granted,[5] the decisions in *Federal Housing Administration* v. *Burr*[6] and *Re-*

---

[1] Coffman, "Legal Status of Government Corporations," 7 *Federal Bar Journal*, 389, 397.

[2] 295 U.S. 229.

[3] *Ibid.*, p. 233.

[4] *Crozier* v. *Krupp*, 224 U.S. 290; *Cramp* v. *Curtis*, 246 U.S. 28; *Wells* v. *Roper*, 246 U.S. 335; and see cases collected in 69 F. Supp. 955.

[5] 39 Op. Atty. Gen. 559, 565.

[6] 309 U.S. 242.

construction Finance Corporation v. *J. G. Menihan Corp.*[1] indicate that an attachment or injunction, where authorized by local law and limited to the single transaction in suit, might be afforded a private litigant. In this connection, it is to be noted that section 264 (d) of the Banking Act of 1933,[2] which incorporates the Federal Deposit Insurance Corporation, provides that no attachment or execution shall issue before final judgment has been rendered.

Laches and Limitations. As a general rule, local statutes of limitations and the equitable defense of laches are not available against the United States.[3] This doctrine was known to the common law and provides a means of better safeguarding, in view of the size and complexity of the governmental organization, rights, and property of the sovereign. Whether this immunity extends to Government corporations is in doubt. In the past the courts have declined to extend such immunity to Government corporations.[4] Two recent well-considered decisions have taken the opposite position, holding these organizations to be integral parts of the Federal Government and subject to the same rules of law.[5] While suit on a claim of a Government corporation might be brought by the United States, as real party in interest [6] and the effect of the statute of limitations possibly avoided, there may nevertheless be many reasons why this solution would be administratively unsatisfactory. If, therefore, exemption from the effects of these defenses is justifiable, provision therefor should be made as was done for the Commodity Credit Corporation, in the charter. Moreover, where the limitation arises by reason of a provision in a contract which the corporation is authorized to

<hr>

[1] 312 U.S. 81.
[2] 48 Stat. 168.
[3] *United States* v. *Summerlin,* 310 U.S. 414.
[4] *Lindgren* v. *Emergency Fleet Corporation,* 55 F. 2d 117; certiorari denied, 286 U.S. 542; *United States* v. *Brown,* 160 N.E. 13 N.Y.; *Reconstruction Finance Corporation* v. *Foster-Wheeler,* 70 F. Supp. 420; *Home Owners' Loan Corporation* v. *Williams,* 168 S.W. 2d 325 (Texas, 1943); 19 Comp. Gen. 537, 542.
[5] *United States* v. *New York Dock Co.,* 100 F. Supp. 303; *Reconstruction Finance Corporation* v. *Marcum,* 100 F. Supp. 953.
[6] *United States* v. *Czarnikow-Rienda,* 40 F. 2d 214; *Russell Wheel & Foundry Co.* v. *United States,* 31 F. 2d 826.

make, the limitation will be effective even if the United States should sue in its own name.[1]

Interest. While, in the absence of a special contract or statute (as in the case of tax refunds), the United States is not required to pay interest upon claims or judgments against it,[2] Government corporations, on the other hand, are still regarded for this purpose as separate entities with a status inferior to that of the sovereign and interest may be included in judgments against them.[3]

Counterclaim and Set-Off. It seems quite clear that in any suit by or against the United States, a set-off involving a claim of or against a Government corporation may be properly interposed. In *Cherry Cotton Mills* v. *United States* [4] the United States, in answering a suit for refund of taxes, interposed a counterclaim based upon a debt due to the Reconstruction Finance Corporation. The counterclaim was permitted, the court saying:

> That the Congress chose to call it a corporation does not alter its characteristics so as to make it something other than what it actually is, an agency selected by the Government to accomplish purely governmental purposes.[5]

It is uncertain whether the converse would be true; i.e., a private litigant being sued by one Government corporation interposing as a counterclaim a cause of action against the United States or another Government corporation.

Costs. Prior to the enactment of Title 28 of the United States Code, effective September 1, 1948, the question of the liability of Government corporations for the payment of court costs on the unsuccessful termination of litigation had been set-

---

[1] *United States* v. *Chicago, Rock Island and Pacific Railroad Co.*, 200 F. 2d 263 (CA 5; 1952).

[2] *United States* v. *Goltra*, 312 U.S. 203; *Thayer West Point Hotel* v. *United States*, 329 U.S. 585.

[3] *National Home for Disabled Volunteers* v. *Parrish*, 229 U.S. 494; *Ferguson* v. *Union National Bank*, 126 F. 2d 753, involving the Federal Housing Administrator who, although not a corporation, may sue and be sued.

[4] 327 U.S. 536.

[5] *Ibid.*, p. 539. To the same effect are the decisions of the Comptroller General reported in 7 Comp. Gen. 186, 576.

tled by the decision of the Supreme Court in *Reconstruction Finance Corporation* v. *J. G. Menihan Corp.*[1] In that case the Reconstruction Finance Corporation, having purchased certain property, including a trademark, pledged as security for a loan, brought suit, unsuccessfully, to enjoin the defendant from using the trademark. In giving judgment, the district court assessed statutory cost and a reasonable allowance against the plaintiff. The Supreme Court affirmed, stating that the right to sue and be sued made the corporation subject to the ordinary incidents of litigation and that waivers of the sovereign immunity would be liberally construed.

Section 2412 (a) of Title 28 of the United States Code, however, provides that:

> The United States shall be liable for fees and costs only when such liability is expressly provided for by Act of Congress.

Although the reference is to the "United States" and Chapter 161, in which the section appears, is entitled "United States as a Party Generally," section 2408 in the same chapter provided that security for costs shall not be required of the United States or *any agency thereof*, and that costs taxable against the United States or *any agency thereof* under *other* acts of Congress shall be paid out of contingent funds. Section 451 defines the term "agency" as including "any corporation in which the United States has a proprietary interest, unless the context shows such term was intended to be used in a more limited sense." The Reviser's Note on section 2412 [2] states that subsection (a) is new but that it follows the well-known common law rule that a sovereign is not liable for costs unless specific provision therefor is made by law. The use of the word "expressly" in the section raises the question as to whether the reasoning of the Supreme Court in *Reconstruction Finance Corporation* v. *J. G. Menihan Corp.*[3] would be applicable to the statute in its present form.

Tort Claims. The Federal Tort Claims Act [4] grants the consent

---

[1] 312 U.S. 81.
[2] H. Rept. 308, 80th Cong., p. A189.
[3] 312 U.S. 81.
[4] Title 28, U.S.C. secs. 1346 (b) and 2671-2680.

of the United States to be sued on claims sounding in tort, with certain exceptions specified in section 2680. It also provides that, notwithstanding the authority of any federal agency to sue and be sued, its provisions shall be, for claims within its cognizance, the exclusive remedy.[1] Under those provisions therefore, the remedy for a negligent tort by a Government corporation would be a suit against the United States.[2] As to those causes of action which are not covered by the Tort Claims Act, one possible inference is that the corporations will continue to be amenable to suit in the same manner as heretofore.

Collateral Proceedings. After a period of uncertainty, the rule is now settled that the authority of the corporation to sue and be sued subjects it to collateral proceedings as well as to suits in which it has a direct interest. In *Federal Housing Administration* v. *Burr* [3] the proceeding was in the nature of a garnishment against the salary of an employee. The Federal Housing Administrator, although not a corporation, is authorized to sue and be sued.[4] This authority, the Supreme Court held, would include the same liability to suit as if the administrator were a private person and he may be required, therefore, in a proceeding instituted by a creditor of one of his employees, to respond in accord with local garnishment statutes.

Execution on Judgment. The authority to sue and be sued, the Supreme Court has held,[5] contemplates the normal incidents of litigation, including the issuance of an execution against the funds and other property of the defendant. Under section 302 of the Government Corporation Control Act, however, Government corporations are required, in the main, to keep their funds in checking accounts with the Treasurer of the United States, where they would not be subject to levy.[6] Their property, on the other hand, would have no such protection and it may be desirable, where

---

[1] *Ibid.,* sec. 2679
[2] *Wickman* v. *Inland Waterways,* 78 F.S. 284; see also *Gardner* v. *Panama Railroad,* District Court Canal Zone, Oct. 7, 1948.
[3] 309 U.S. 242.
[4] 12 U.S.C. sec. 1702.
[5] *Federal Housing Administration* v. *Burr,* 309 U.S. 242.
[6] *Buchanan* v. *Alexander,* 4 How. 20.

the need is indicated, to limit the effect of the "sue and be sued" clause by forbidding a levy upon corporate property, as was done in the charter of the Commodity Credit Corporation.[1]

Suits in Foreign Courts. The effect of the "sue and be sued" clause in foreign courts, as contrasted with its effect in the courts of this nation, cannot be accurately predicted. In cases where corporations owned by foreign countries are sued in courts in the United States, the current rule is that, if the State Department certifies that the foreign government corporation defendant is entitled to enjoy diplomatic immunity, the courts of this country must yield to that advice.[2] The soundness of this rule has been questioned as an invasion of the judicial function [3] and the proposal made that the Secretary of State confine himself in all cases, as he did in some,[4] to a mere transmittal of the claim of sovereign immunity and a "suggestion" that the claim be considered by the court.

The rules in foreign courts, where settled, would undoubtedly vary between these extremes from country to country, or might, on the other hand, be based upon comity. It would be difficult, therefore, to determine in advance what would be the decision of a foreign court with respect to a corporation owned by the United States.

Penalty Mail

Suggested Language

(*j*) *To use the United States mails in the same manner and under the same conditions as the executive department of the Federal Government.*

---

[1] P.L. 805, 80th Cong.

[2] *United States of Mexico* v. *Schmuck,* 293 N.Y. 264, 56 N.E. 2d 577; *The Navemar,* 303 U.S. 68, 74; *Ex parte Republic of Peru,* 318 U.S. 578; *United States* v. *Deutsches K. G. et al.,* 31 F. 2d 199 (1929); *Miller et al.* v. *Ferrocaril del Pacifico de Nicaragua,* 131 Me. 251, 18 A. 2d 688 (1941).

[3] A. K. Kuhn, 39 *American Journal of International Law,* 772.

[4] *Hannes* v. *Kingdom of Roumania Monopolies Institute,* 260 App. Div. 189, 20 N.Y. Supp. 2d 825 (1940); *Lamont* v. *Travelers Insurance Company,* 281 N.Y. 362 24 N.E. 2d 81 (1939); see also 27 *Michigan Law Review* 751 and 50 *Yale Law Journal* 1088.

Comment

The authority of the executive departments to use the mails goes back to 1877,[1] and the custom of extending this privilege to Government corporations, as administrative agencies of the United States, is well established. The Penalty Mail Act of 1948 [2] while it repealed the act of June 28, 1944,[3] which had required payment for mail transported, did not by its terms authorize the use of the mails by Government corporations and the suggested language should be included to accomplish this purpose.

Instruments

Suggested Language

(k) *To execute, in accordance with its by-laws, all instruments necessary or appropriate in the exercise of any of its powers.*

Comment

This power is probably included by inference in the provisions authorizing the corporation to make contracts, to expend its funds and to dispose of its property. Nevertheless it appears useful to grant it in specific terms and thereby to provide unquestionable authority for the corporation to designate, by its by-laws, the officers or other agents who shall execute instruments on its behalf.

Incidental Power

Suggested Language

(l) *To take such actions as may be necessary or appropriate to carry out the powers herein or hereafter specifically conferred upon it:* provided, *that the corporation shall undertake no new types of activities not included in the annual budget program.*

Comment

Obviously, it is impossible to foresee with complete accuracy every type of authority for which a need may arise. The custom,

---

[1] 39 U.S.C. sec. 321, 19 Stat. 335.
[2] 62 Stat. 1048.
[3] 39 U.S.C. sec. 321c-e.

therefore, of including in corporate charters a power in these general terms has proved useful where the action which needs to be taken might not fit clearly within any of the general powers expressly conferred. It indicates, moreover, an intention on the part of the creator of the corporation that the powers expressly conferred be construed with reasonable flexibility. The language suggested, it should be noted, does not purport to confer additional powers on the corporation, but confers merely one additional power: viz., to do such particular *things* as may be necessary or proper in connection with clearly authorized activities.

4. Specific Powers

Introductory

Suggested Language

Sec. 5. Subject to the provisions of the Government Corporation Control Act, the corporation shall have and may exercise the following specific powers, in addition to those elsewhere conferred in this article:

Comment

The specific powers constitute the substantive program of the corporation. Examples of specific powers are the authority to construct, maintain, and operate a railroad, to make loans, to support the prices of agricultural commodities, etc. Such specific powers must be exercised subject to the provisions of the Government Corporation Control Act, and plans for the use of the powers must be included in the annual budget program submitted to the Congress.

Where it is necessary to grant powers to a corporation in very broad and general terms, it may be useful to add a proviso that "the corporation shall undertake no new types of activities not included in the annual budget program prescribed by section 102 of the Government Corporation Control Act." The word "activity" is defined in section 102 as "major types of activities." This proviso would insure prior congressional consideration of any major new undertakings.

5. Management

Suggested Language

Sec. 6(a). The management of the corporation shall be vested in an administrator to be appointed by the President, by and with the advice and consent of the Senate, and who shall receive compensation at the rate of $____ per annum.

(b) To assist the administrator in the execution of the functions vested in the corporation there shall be a deputy administrator who shall be appointed by the President, by and with the advice and consent of the Senate, and who shall receive compensation at the rate of $____ per annum. The deputy administrator shall perform such duties as the administrator may from time to time designate, and shall be acting administrator and perform the functions of the administrator during the absence or disability of the administrator or in the event of a vacancy in the office of the administrator.

(c) There is hereby established the Advisory Board of the _____ Corporation, which shall be composed of five members appointed by the President. The Advisory Board shall meet at the call of the administrator, who shall require it to meet not less often than once each ____ days; shall review the general policies of the corporation; and shall advise the administrator with respect thereto. Members of the Advisory Board shall receive for their services as members compensation of not to exceed $50 per diem when actually engaged in the performance of their duties, together with their necessary traveling expenses while going to and coming from meetings.

OR

Sec. 6. The management of the corporation shall be vested in a Board of Directors consisting of not less than ____ nor more

48

than ____ persons who shall be appointed by the supervisory official, or if he so elects, consisting of the supervisory official and ____ to ____ other persons. One of the directors shall be designated by the supervisory official as chairman of the board. The directors shall receive no salary for their services on the board, but under regulations and in amounts prescribed by the board, with the approval of the supervisory official, may be paid a reasonable per diem allowance in lieu of subsistence in connection with attendance at meetings of the board or in connection with time spent on special service of the corporation, and their traveling expenses to and from meetings or when upon special service, without regard to the Subsistence Expense Act of 1926, or the Standardized Government Travel Regulations. Nothing contained in this article or in any other act shall be construed to prevent the appointment and service, as director, officer, or employee of the corporation, of any officer or employee of the United States serving without extra compensation therefor. The directors, of whom ____ shall constitute a quorum for the transaction of business, shall meet for organization purposes when and where called by the supervisory official, and subsequent meetings as provided by the by-laws.

Comment

Form of Management. There is no standard pattern for the organization and management of a Government corporation. As in the case of any other governmental activity, the management can and does vary with the nature of the function to be performed, the relationship of the corporation to established departments and other special circumstances. The suggested language is designed merely to illustrate two rather common forms of management.

Board of Directors. A board of directors is not an indispensable attribute of a Government corporation. While the management of a corporation is generally vested in a board of directors, in the case of at least three corporations—the Inland Waterways Corporation, Reconstruction Finance Corporation, and the Public

Housing Administration (formerly the U. S. Housing Authority)—management is vested in a single head.

The board of directors of a private corporation represents the stockholder-owners. The directors, individually and collectively, are primarily responsible, by law, for the management of the business and may be held responsible for any breach of their trust relationship to the corporation. The board's mission may be broadly defined as consisting of (1) the formulation of basic policies; (2) the selection of executive officers to operate the business; and (3) general supervision to assure that operations are being directed toward the accomplishment of the adopted policies.

While the functions of both private and Government boards of directors are roughly analogous, it must be recognized that there are extremely important differences. A Government corporation, unlike a private corporation, is merely one cog in a very complex machine. If the machine is to operate smoothly and not break down, someone must see that all of the cogs are properly meshed together. Therefore, the board of a Government corporation cannot be given the same freedom of action as the board of a private corporation. Corporate policies must be amenable to the policies laid down by the supervisory official, if any, the President, and the Congress, and, where essential, changed or modified to secure over-all consistency. In reviewing and approving the annual budgets submitted by the various corporations, the Congress, in fact, establishes basic policies and performs a function ordinarily assigned to the board of directors of a private corporation. The Government corporation board must of necessity operate within a far more circumscribed area than its private prototype.

The very significant differences between private and Government boards of directors should be taken into consideration, and the advantages and disadvantages of a board versus a single head carefully weighed before a decision is made as to the most suitable form of organization for a given corporation. If the decision is made in favor of a board of directors, additional study is needed to determine the type of board most likely to promote effective administration of the program. Government corporation boards of directors come in all sizes, shapes, and varieties. Boards, for example, may consist of officials of a single department, representatives of several departments, private individuals and public officials, or exclusively private individuals. They may vary in size from three to thirteen members. The actual number of members is open since there is no federal incorporation law which makes provision for them. Boards may meet biannually, quarterly, weekly, or sit full time. Other differences are noted in the discussion below.

Full-Time versus Part-Time Board. One of the most crucial issues is whether board members are to serve full time or part time. If the board is to concern itself exclusively with matters of broad policy and general supervision, a part-time board is indicated. If the board is to be in fact the operating head of the organization, it should be composed of full-time members. Most Government corporation boards are of the former type, but a few have assumed administrative functions ordinarily delegated to a president or general manager in a private corporation.

Experience indicates that the use of a full-time board is subject to a number of serious weaknesses. A full-time board may become so enmeshed in the details of administration that its primary responsibilities, policy formulation and general supervision, may be partly or wholly neglected. The editor, summarizing certain points in a study of boards of directors of private corporations, concluded that "directors, either individually or as a group, cannot participate directly in the multitude of functions required to operate effectively the business of a corporation, although the law typically states that the board of directors shall 'manage' the corporation. Rather the board must direct the management of the corporation's affairs, in a practical sense, by delegating operations to the executive organization to which it has given authority and to which instructions have been provided." [1]

Appointment of Board Members. Where the functions of a corporation fall within the sphere of an established department

[1] M. T. Copeland and A. R. Towl, *The Board of Directors and Business Management* (Cambridge: Harvard University Press, 1947).

and are administratively placed within it, the department head should appoint the board of directors. If the department head is to be held accountable for the proper administration of the corporation, he must possess the same authority with respect to the board as he has with respect to the head or heads of any other activity within his department. The appointments should be directed to be made "without regard to the provisions of the Civil Service laws regarding appointment and removal."

If the corporation is to be wholly independent of established agencies of the executive branch, appointments should be made by the President, by and with the advice and consent of the Senate.

Under the provisions of Article II, Section 2 of the Constitution, appointment of inferior officers of the United States may be vested by the Congress "in the President alone, in the Courts of Law, or in the heads of Departments." Authority to appoint directors, therefore, cannot be vested in persons or groups outside of the Federal Government. President Coolidge in 1928 vetoed a bill to establish a Federal Farm Board on the grounds that a provision requiring him to appoint board members from lists prepared by state officials, cooperative associations, and other nonfederal organizations was contrary to the express provisions of the Constitution.[1]

Chairman of Board. If there is to be a chairman of the board—and for convenience there should be a permanent presiding officer—the charter should provide for the position and prescribe a method for making the designation. Generally, if the department head is named as a member of the board, he also serves as chairman; or if he is not a member, he is authorized to designate the chairman. Authority for the designation of the chairman should be expressly set forth since, in the absence thereof, the power to appoint directors would not imply the right to designate one of the appointees to a position superior to the others.

Qualifications of Directors. If the program of the corporation calls for any unusual qualifications on the part of its directors, those qualifications should be clearly set forth in the charter so

---

[1] 69 *Cong. Rec.*, p. 9530.

that the appointing power will be on notice to give adequate consideration to them in choosing his appointees. Various qualifications may be attached to board membership such as experience, residence in a particular region, political affiliation, or representation of a particular economic group.

In the appointment of some boards and commissions political bipartisanship—as distinguished from nonpartisanship—has been prescribed. This type of board membership, however, would seem to be inappropriate for a Government corporation.

If federal officials are to be ex officio members, or eligible for appointments as board members, the charter should so provide. The dual compensation statutes,[1] unless specifically excepted, would of course apply.

Term of Office. In cases where the corporation is placed within the administrative organization and made subject to the general supervision of an established department, it would not appear to be advisable to fix a term of office for its directors, since the power to remove is, in the absence of statutory provision to the contrary, an incident of the power to appoint.[2] As a matter of public notice, however, it seems desirable to make their tenure expressly dependent upon the "pleasure" of the appointing official. In the case of officials appointed by the President, the rule is well settled that, except in the cases of members of certain quasi-legislative or quasi-judicial bodies,[3] the President has plenary power to remove them.[4]

Compensation. Where the board is made up of full-time officials, the question of their compensation can be determined by a provision in the charter for a specific amount or by authorizing the head of the department to fix the amount. In the case of ex officio members or part-time members, the payment of salary for the discharge of duties as a director would not ordinarily be

---

[1] 5 U.S.C. 58, prohibiting double salaries totaling $2,000; 5 U.S.C. 62, prohibiting any person who holds an office with annual compensation of $2,500 or over from holding other lucrative offices; and 5 U.S.C. 70, prohibiting receipt of extra allowances.

[2] *Burnap* v. *United States*, 252 U.S. 512.

[3] *Humphrey's Executor* v. *United States*, 295 U.S. 602.

[4] *Myers* v. *United States*, 272 U.S. 52; *Morgan* v. *Tennessee Valley Authority*, 115 F. 2d 990, certiorari denied, 312 U.S. 701.

involved. In those cases, however, provision should be made for the payment of traveling and other expenses, including a per diem allowance in lieu of subsistence.

Quorum. The provision for a quorum should be based upon the expected needs of the corporation. Any unusual quorum requirements should be set forth explicitly in the charter, since in the absence of an appropriate provision, the general rule, which requires a majority for a quorum and action by a majority of the quorum, would apply.[1]

Directors as Officers. As a result of their study of private corporations, Copeland and Towl reached the conclusion that "A director should not trespass on the functions of the executives. In the operating field, if a corporation is to be conducted successfully, the initiative must be left to the executive branch of the organization. The opportunities for directors to take initiative are in such matters as assuring adequate provision for succession in management, promoting the adoption of progressive policies, and checking up on results."[2] If a director is to perform executive functions, he should be made an officer of the corporation. In view of the basically different functions assigned to the board of directors and executive staff, it would seem that the dual status of director and officer ought to be avoided, except possibly in the case of one or two of the top executive officers. The presidents of most Government corporations are also directors. However, if such duality is to be permitted, a provision to that effect should be included in the charter.

Executive Staff. The general incorporation laws of the states usually provide for a skeleton group of officers, including a president, a secretary, and a treasurer. In a Government corporation it is customary to grant to the directors the power to appoint "such officers as may be appropriate" and to "prescribe their powers and duties." Where the corporation is an integral part or a close adjunct of another agency, it is usually desirable to prescribe in the charter that the head of such agency shall be the president of the corporation. The Governor of the Canal Zone is,

[1] Fletcher, 2 *Cyclopedia of the Law of Private Corporations,* 204, 210.
[2] Copeland and Towl, *op. cit.,* p. 141.

for example, the President of the Panama Canal Company, and the Director of the Federal Bureau of Prisons is also the head of Federal Prison Industries, Inc. Any other administrative arrangement would diffuse authority and responsibility and might lead to serious conflicts.

Some Government corporation charters place the authority to appoint officers and employees and to prescribe their duties in the department head rather than in the directors.

Other factors to be considered in connection with the appointment of officers are discussed in the section under "General Powers" dealing with "employees, attorneys, and agents."

6. Financing

Suggested Language

Sec. 7 (a). To carry out the functions authorized by this act, there is authorized to be established in the Treasury of the United States a _____ Fund (referred to hereinafter as the "fund"). The capital of the fund shall consist of such amounts as may be advanced to it for appropriations, together with the value of assets transferred to the fund, less the liabilities assumed, at the beginning of its operations. The value of assets transferred shall be determined by the corporation, taking into consideration original cost, less depreciation, the usable value to the transferee if clearly less than cost, obsolete and unusable inventories and other reasonably determinable shrinkages in values.

(b) Such sums as may be required are authorized to be appropriated without fiscal year limitations. Advances shall be made to the fund from the appropriations made therefor when requested by the corporation.

(c) The corporation shall pay into miscellaneous receipts of the Treasury at the close of each fiscal year interest on the capital of the fund at a rate determined by the Secretary of the Treasury, taking into consideration the average rate on outstanding interest-bearing marketable public debt obligations of the United States.

(d) Whenever any capital in the fund is determined by the corporation to be in excess of its current needs, such capital shall be credited to the appropriation from which advanced where it shall be held for future advances.

(e) Receipts from any operations under this act shall be credited to the fund. The fund shall be available for payment of all expenditures of the corporation under this act.

56

(f) Appropriations are hereby authorized for payment to the corporation of such amounts as may be shown in the annual budget program of the corporation as necessary to cover actual losses of prior years sustained in the conduct of its activities. Amounts appropriated to the corporation under authority of this subsection shall not be added to the amount of advances and shall not require payment of interest under subsection (c) of this section.

Comment

A very great part of the difference between a corporation and an agency arises from the method of financing its operations. The suggested language differs from that found in existing corporate charters. The changes are in draftsmanship and procedure rather than in substance. The new language was developed by the Treasury and the Bureau of the Budget.

The appropriations are equivalent to the corporation's line of credit. When the corporation draws upon its line of credit, the money is transferred to fund. Interest is paid upon the outstanding amount of money transferred from the appropriation to the fund. The amount of advances subject to interest is reduced by the amount of any repayments to the appropriation. Such repayments are credited to the appropriation and are available for future advances when required by the corporation.

Most corporations receive substantial revenues from the goods and services they furnish to customers. The language authorizes the corporation to control and use and reuse its revenue for any authorized purpose including construction and capital expansion. Receipts are credited to the fund and are available for expenditure as the management may direct within the legal authority of the corporation.

A corporation derives much of its flexibility from the fact that it does not operate out of direct appropriations. Direct appropriations can be made to a corporation, but experience indicates that the intermingling of corporate and appropriated funds should be avoided. The use of direct appropriations may unnecessarily restrict corporate flexibility. Money transferred to the fund from either appropriations or receipts does not have the legal status of appropriated funds.

Much of the financial flexibility of a corporation can be obtained by the creation of a revolving fund without necessarily establishing a "body corporate."

Government Investment

The Government's investment in a corporation consists of two elements: (1) cash advanced from appropriations; and (2) properties and other assets transferred to the corporation. The determination of the amount of the Government's "investment" is extremely important because it controls the amount of interest which the corporation must pay to the Treasury. The purpose is to arrive at a figure fairly representing the net investment of the United States, both in cash and other assets, in the enterprise. Therefore, the valuation of any assets transferred to the corporation is based primarily on original cost, less depreciation, rather than on cost of reproduction or current market value.

The valuation of properties and assets may present peculiarly difficult problems, particularly when the corporation is taking over an existing enterprise. Allowance may have to be made for properties which are obsolete or which have a usable value to the corporation which is clearly less than cost. In the case of defense related projects, allowance may have to be made for facilities which are required for defense, although not essential for the conduct of strictly commercial operations. The Panama Railroad Company charter, for example, provides that "there shall be excluded from such amount any portion of the transferred property which is properly allocable to defense." Special protective facilities or facilities utilized exclusively by the military may be readily classified in the "defense" category. It is a far more complex problem to ascertain the portion properly allocable to defense in the case of common-user facilities. The additional costs allocable to defense may consist of excess plant capacity, more costly equipment than would be required for normal commercial operations, modification of designs and specifications to meet military requirements, etc. No general formula can be prescribed,

and language should be developed after careful study to meet
the problems peculiar to the enterprise under consideration.

Allocation of Costs

The allocation of costs on assets transferred to the corporation
is discussed above. In the case of enterprises which are required
to carry on certain nonrevenue-producing or defense activities,
it may be desirable to include in the charter language governing
the allocation of both capital and operating costs. Capital costs
allocated to nonrevenue-producing or defense facilities are usually
deducted from the amount of the Government's investment subject to interest and are excluded from the corporation's rate base.
Provision may also have to be made for annual grants to the
corporation to cover the cost of operating such facilities. No
language is suggested because no two corporations are likely to
have comparable problems.

Provisions authorizing the allocation of capital costs among
two or more functions are found in the charters of the Tennessee
Valley Authority and the Panama Canal Company. The Congress,
in addition, recognized the special role of the Panama Canal in
defense by excluding interest during the construction period
from the capital investment. The charter of the Virgin Islands
Corporation authorizes annual grants to the corporation to meet
expenses of nonrevenue-producing programs.

7. Miscellaneous Provisions

There are, in addition to the foregoing elements, some additional general provisions which would be appropriate to the charters of most Government corporations and a few special provisions which some corporations, by reason of their program needs or the circumstances of their organization, may find either necessary or useful.

Reserved Right to Amend or Repeal

Suggested Language

Sec. ___. *The right to alter, amend, or repeal this charter is expressly reserved.*

Comment

Although the entire ownership of the corporation would be in the United States and no claim, therefore, could be made that a contract had been created between the Government and the stockholders, as was the case in *Dartmouth College* v. *Woodward*,[1] it may nevertheless be useful to include a warning of nature in the corporate charter. One of the advantages in the Government's use of the corporate form lies in the familiarity of the commercial public with private corporations. The same psychological relationship would seem to require notice to that public that the status and powers of the corporation could be modified or abolished at the will of the Congress.

---

[1] 4 Wheat. 518.

Inclusion in the Government Corporation Control Act

Suggested Language

Sec. ___. *Section 101 of the Government Corporation Control Act is hereby amended by inserting therein the words "_____ [name of corporation] _____."*

Comment

Since it appears to be intended that all corporations hereafter organized shall operate within the terms of the Government Corporation Control Act, it is suggested that, to assure coverage, the charter contain a provision amending section 101 of the Government Corporation Control Act of 1945 to include the name of the corporation.

Priority of Debts

Suggested Language

Sec. ___. *To have, in the payment of debts out of bankrupt, insolvent, or decedent's estates, the priority of the United States.*

Comment

Notwithstanding the steady increase in the identification of Government corporations with other administrative arms of the Government, it is doubtful whether the process has reached the point where the debts due the corporations will be accorded the priority afforded by 31 U.S.C. sec. 191 to the debts due the United States. In the early days of Government corporations, the decision on this question, based upon the "separate entity" concept, was clearly in the negative.[1] The question was again directly raised recently in *Reconstruction Finance Corporation* v. *Brady,*[2] and the claim of priority was again denied although the decision was made on other grounds.

If, therefore, controlling considerations of policy indicate that the Government corporation should be permitted to invoke the priority of the United States in order to conserve its funds,[3] this

---

[1] *Sloan Shipyards* v. *Emergency Fleet Corporation,* 258 U.S. 549, 570.
[2] 150 S.W. 2d 357 (Texas, 1941).
[3] See *United States* v. *Emory,* 314 U.S. 423.

provision should be included. The use of the word "bankrupt" would be intended to extend its effect to estates which, although not actually insolvent, may be under administration pursuant to one of the bankruptcy laws; the adjective "insolvent" would cover those under state statutes and, finally, the inclusion of the descriptive word "decedents" might serve to dispense with all or part of the waiting period generally prescribed in the probate courts for the payment of claims against estates subject to their jurisdiction.

Taxation

The property of the Federal Government, to the full extent of the Government's interest therein, is immune from taxation not consented to.[1] The property of Government corporations has also been held to be immune, even in the absence of statutory exemption, on the ground that the beneficial ownership of such property is in the United States and that any burden upon it would be a burden on the activities of the Federal Government.[2]

Although Government corporations are not subject to taxation, the impact of their tax-free operations on the local structure in some instances might make it desirable that steps be taken to bridge the gap. In those cases it is suggested that a provision be included in the charter authorizing the corporation to make payments *in lieu of* taxes. The scope of this authorization may be expanded or limited as the situation warrants, but the final determination of which taxes should be compensated for, and the method of determining the amount of such payments, should be determined by the Congress in the charter or, possibly, delegated to the corporation. It would also serve to avoid imposing liability on the corporation for any interest and penalties that might be attached to the liability for taxes.

If, on the other hand, the corporation were simply made "subject to taxes" or to certain taxes, as for example, taxes on real property, a situation might develop in which, by reason of differ-

---

[1] *United States* v. *Alleghany County,* 322 U.S. 174.

[2] *Clallam County* v. *United States,* 263 U.S. 341; *United States* v. *City of Philadelphia,* 140 F. 2d 406; see also cases cited in footnote to *Reconstruction Finance Corporation* v. *Beaver County,* 328 U.S. 204 at p. 206.

ing local interpretations, the corporation may be unable to predict its tax liability or it may by reason of an unexpected interpretation be unduly burdened in carrying on its activities in a region where its policy requires that it operate.

The Reconstruction Finance Corporation, in section 10 of its old charter,[1] was made subject to taxes on its real property. In Pennsylvania, where the corporation installed some machinery for war work, the assessment levied by local authority on the machinery as real property was upheld by the Supreme Court on the ground that, under the language of the corporate charter, the local definition of "real property" was binding on the corporation.[2] As a consequence, the corporation, in preparing its new charter,[3] inserted a provision [4] designed to restrict the taxability of its property, and providing specifically that:

. . . possessory interests, pipe lines, power lines, or machinery or equipment owned by the Corporation regardless of their nature, use, or manner of attachment or affixation to the land, building, or other structure upon or in which the same may be located, . . .[5]

shall not be taxable. This method may or may not dispose of the problem with respect to the items enumerated, but the type of property next made the subject of adjudication might be chattels real, or some other unusual property interest which might, under conflicting interpretations, present the corporation with difficult problems in administration or finance. Clearly, it would not be feasible to amend the charter each time a new situation arises, nor would such amendments be likely to enable the corporation to avoid payment of taxes theretofore validly assessed.

The method of computing payments in lieu of taxes should take into consideration the benefits derived by the locality from the federal activity. The formula directed to be followed on low-cost housing projects [6] sets forth many of the factors which should

---

[1] 15 U.S.C. sec. 610.

[2] *Reconstruction Finance Corporation* v. *Beaver County*, 328 U.S. 204.

[3] Act of June 30, 1947, 61 Stat. 202, 205.

[4] Subsequently eliminated by section 5 of the act of May 25, 1948, 62 Stat. 261, 265.

[5] Sec. 8.

[6] 40 U.S.C. sec. 422.

be taken into consideration and may be used as a starting model. In addition, where the determination is directed to be made by the corporate authority or by the head of the supervisory department, such determination should be specifically declared to be "not reviewable" to avoid appeals to the local courts for judicial review under section 10 of the Administrative Procedure Act.[1]

Unauthorized Use of Corporate Name

The state systems for organization of private corporations generally protect existing corporations from having their corporate names improperly taken by subsequent applicants' articles of incorporation. Since Government corporations may carry on their activities anywhere in the United States without qualifying under the laws of the various states, it would seem appropriate to include a provision in the charter prohibiting and making a misdemeanor the unauthorized use of the corporate name or of any name so closely similar as to be likely to mislead.

Utilization of Other Governmental Services

To clarify the status of the corporation as an administrative segment of the Federal Government, it may be well to include a provision authorizing the corporation, with the consent of the head of any department, agency, or independent establishment of the Government, to avail itself of the use of information, services, facilities, officers, or employees of such agency in the discharge of its authorized corporate activities. To the extent that such services are sought under circumstances that would justify reimbursement, section 601 of the Economy Act of 1932[2] and the general power of the corporation to make contracts would be authorization for such arrangements. As a general rule, a corporation should be required to reimburse other government agencies for services rendered to it.

It is now accepted practice to include a provision in the charter requiring the corporation to reimburse the Civil Service retirement fund for Government contributions to the retirement fund

---

[1] 5 U.S.C. sec. 1009.
[2] 31 U.S.C. sec. 686.

applicable to its employees, and the Employees' Compensation Fund for any benefit payments made on behalf of its employees.

Liquidation

Wherever possible, provision should be made in the corporate charter for a method of liquidation upon the termination of the corporation's existence. It is suggested that a limited period, depending upon the type of activity, be given to the management to liquidate or transfer the assets and that, at the end of such period, the task be transferred to the supervising agency or to such other agency of the Government as may be appropriate.

PART III. AUTHORITY TO CREATE GOVERNMENT CORPORATIONS

8. Method of Formation

The foregoing discussion of the form of charter for Government corporations has been concerned with corporation charters enacted by the Congress as general statutes. This method of creation is the one that would normally be expected to be followed and the one that is generally considered preferable.

In the past, however, there have been instances where the Congress, instead of creating certain corporations by its own legislative act, has authorized, in legislation dealing broadly with some area of national interest, the creation of a Government corporation in connection with the program adopted. Section 11 of the act of September 7, 1916,[1] creating the United States Shipping Board, authorized that board to form one or more corporations under the laws of the District of Columbia and, accordingly, it organized the Emergency Fleet Corporation. Again, in an appropriation for war housing during World War I,[2] the President was authorized to create a corporation, and he utilized his authority to have the United States Housing Corporation organized under the general corporation laws of the State of New York. The years 1933–1938 saw a number of Government corporations organized under the laws of the various states pursuant to more or less clear statutory authority.[3]

Section 304(b) of the Government Corporation Control Act,

---

[1] 39 Stat. 731.
[2] 40 Stat. 595.
[3] See *Handbook of Government Corporations,* prepared by the General Accounting Office in 1945, and published as S. Doc. 86, 79th Cong.

in directing the dissolution of Government corporations organized under state laws, implies disapproval of the further use of this method of incorporation.

It would seem to follow, therefore, that where the Congress sees a need to grant advance authority for a federal official to organize a corporation, as was done in the Foreign Assistance Act of 1948 and the Rubber Act of 1948, and does not specifically authorize the charter under the laws of a state or territory, its policy would favor creation either by executive order or other similar federal document.

Since the mere inclusion in a statute of authority to create a Government corporation would not be, in and of itself, sufficient to permit the establishment of a corporation with adequate powers and flexibility, or to provide for its financing and control, the document of creation should follow the general lines and be shaped by the same general considerations that would determine the form of a corporate charter enacted by the Congress. To accomplish this purpose, it is suggested that in any legislative provision authorizing the creation of a corporation, there should be contained a grant of the minimum necessary powers and conditions to enable the corporation to carry on its operations and to function smoothly within the governmental organization. Furthermore, to avoid the situation which existed in the past with respect to certain corporations, when their very existence was doubtful or unknown, it is suggested that these minimum conditions include provisions for filing the charters with the Federal Register and in such other places as may seem desirable.

It is suggested, therefore, that the following language which is similar to that employed in the Foreign Assistance Act of 1948 and the Rubber Act of 1948 be used in any legislative provision designed to authorize the creation of a Government corporation:

Sec. __ (a) The President is hereby authorized and empowered to create a corporation for the purpose of _____ .

    (b) Any corporation created under this section
        (1) shall have the power to sue and be sued; to

acquire, hold and dispose of property; to use its revenue, to determine the character of and necessity for its obligations and expenditures and the manner in which they shall be incurred, allowed, and paid, subject to provisions of law applicable to Government corporations, and to exercise such other powers as may be necessary or appropriate to carry out the purposes of such corporation;

(2) shall have its powers set out in a charter (certified copies of which shall be filed with the Secretary of the Senate and the Clerk of the House of Representatives) and which shall be published in the Federal Register, all amendments to which shall be similarly (filed and) published;

(3) shall not have succession beyond June 30, 19___, except for purposes of liquidation, unless its life is extended beyond such date pursuant to act of Congress; and

(4) shall be subject to the Government Corporation Control Act to the same extent as wholly owned Government corporations listed in section 101 of said act.

(c) [A provision providing either for appropriations to a fund, or authority to borrow from the Treasury.]

APPENDIX

Government Corporation Control Act [1]

PUBLIC LAW 248–79TH CONGRESS
CHAPTER 557–1ST SESSION

AN ACT

To provide for financial control of Government corporations.

Be it enacted by the Senate and House of Representatives of the United States of America in Congress assembled, That this Act may be cited as the "Government Corporation Control Act."

DECLARATION OF POLICY

SEC. 2. It is hereby declared to be the policy of the Congress to bring Government corporations and their transactions and operations under annual scrutiny by the Congress and provide current financial control thereof.

TITLE I—Wholly Owned Government Corporations

SEC. 101. As used in this Act the term "wholly owned Government corporation" means the Commodity Credit Corporation; Federal Intermediate Credit Banks; Production Credit Corporations; Regional Agricultural Credit Corporations; Farmers Home Corporation; Federal Crop Insurance Corporation; Federal Farm Mortgage Corporation; Federal Surplus Commodities Corporation; Reconstruction Finance Corporation; Defense Plant Corpo-

---

[1] 59 Stat. 597.

71

ration; Defense Supplies Corporation; Metals Reserve Company; Rubber Reserve Company; War Damage Corporation; Federal National Mortgage Association; the RFC Mortgage Company; Disaster Loan Corporation; Inland Waterways Corporation; Warrior River Terminal Company; The Virgin Islands Company; Federal Prison Industries, Incorporated; United States Spruce Production Corporation; Institute of Inter-American Affairs; Institute of Inter-American Transportation; Inter-American Educational Foundation, Incorporated; Inter-American Navigation Corporation; Prencinradio, Incorporated; Cargoes, Incorporated; Export-Import Bank of Washington; Petroleum Reserves Corporation; Rubber Development Corporation; U. S. Commercial Company; Smaller War Plants Corporation; Federal Public Housing Authority (or United States Housing Authority) and including public housing projects financed from appropriated funds and operations thereof; Defense Homes Corporation; Federal Savings and Loan Insurance Corporation; Home Owners' Loan Corporation; United States Housing Corporation; Panama Railroad Company; Tennessee Valley Authority; Federal Housing Administration; and Tennessee Valley Associated Cooperatives, Incorporated.

SEC. 102. Each wholly owned Government corporation shall cause to be prepared annually a business-type budget which shall be submitted to the Bureau of the Budget, under such rules and regulations as the President may establish as to the date of submission, the form and content, the classification of data,[1] and the manner in which such budget program shall be prepared and presented. The budget program shall be a business-type budget, or plan of operations, with due allowance given to the need for flexibility, including provision for emergencies and contingencies, in order that the corporation may properly carry out its activities as authorized by law. The budget program shall contain estimates of the financial condition and operations of the corporation for the current and ensuing fiscal years and the actual condition and results of operation for the last completed fiscal year.

---

[1] As amended by sec. 105 of the Budgeting and Accounting Procedures Act of 1950.

Such budget program shall include a statement of financial condition, a statement of income and expense, an analysis of surplus or deficit, a statement of sources and application of funds, and such other supplementary statements and information as are necessary or desirable to make known the financial condition and operations of the corporation. Such statement shall include estimates of operations by major types of activities, together with estimates of administrative expenses, estimates of borrowings, and estimates of the amount of Government capital funds which shall be returned to the Treasury during the fiscal year or the appropriations required to provide for the restoration of capital impairments.

SEC. 103. The budget programs of the corporations as modified, amended, or revised by the President shall be transmitted to the Congress as a part of the annual Budget required by the Budget and Accounting Act, 1921. Amendments to the annual budget programs may be submitted from time to time.

Budget programs shall be submitted for all wholly owned Government corporations covering operations for the fiscal year commencing July 1, 1946, and each fiscal year thereafter.

SEC. 104. The budget programs transmitted by the President to the Congress shall be considered and legislation shall be enacted making necessary appropriations, as may be authorized by law, making available for expenditure for operating and administrative expenses such corporate funds or other financial resources or limiting the use thereof as the Congress may determine and providing for repayment of capital funds and the payment of dividends. The provisions of this section shall not be construed as preventing Government corporations from carrying out and financing their activities as authorized by existing law, nor as affecting the provisions of section 26 of the Tennessee Valley Authority Act, as amended. The provisions of this section shall not be construed as affecting the existing authority of any Government corporation to make contracts or other commitments without reference to fiscal year limitations.[1]

---

[1] As amended by P.L. 268, 80th Cong.

SEC. 105. The financial transactions of wholly owned Government corporations shall be audited by the General Accounting Office in accordance with the principles and procedures applicable to commercial corporate transactions and under such rules and regulations as may be prescribed by the Comptroller General of the United States: *Provided,* That such rules and regulations may provide for the retention at the offices of such corporations, in whole or in part, of any accounts of accountable officers, covering corporate financial transactions, which are required by existing law to be settled and adjusted in the General Accounting Office, and for the settlement and adjustment of such accounts in whole or in part upon the basis of examinations in the course of the audit herein provided, but nothing in this proviso shall be construed as affecting the powers reserved to the Tennessee Valley Authority in section 831h (b) of Title 16. The audit shall be conducted at the place or places where the accounts of the respective corporations are normally kept. The representatives of the General Accounting Office shall have access to all books, accounts, financial records, reports, files, and all other papers, things, or property belonging to or in use by the respective corporations and necessary to facilitate the audit, and they shall be afforded full facilities for verifying transactions with the balances or securities held by depositaries, fiscal agents, and custodians. The audit shall begin with the first fiscal year commencing after the enactment of this Act.

SEC. 106. A report of each such audit for each fiscal year ending on June 30 shall be made by the Comptroller General to the Congress not later than January 15 following the close of the fiscal year for which such audit is made. The report shall set forth the scope of the audit and shall include a statement (showing intercorporate relations) of assets and liabilities, capital and surplus or deficit; a statement of surplus or deficit analysis; a statement of income and expense; a statement of sources and application of funds; and such comments and information as may be deemed necessary to keep Congress informed of the operations and financial condition of the several corporations, together with such recommendations with respect thereto as the Comptroller

General may deem advisable, including a report of any impairment of capital noted in the audit and recommendations for the return of such Government capital or the payment of such dividends as, in his judgment, should be accomplished. The report shall also show specifically any program, expenditure, or other financial transaction or undertaking observed in the course of the audit which, in the opinion of the Comptroller General, has been carried on or made without authority of law. A copy of each report shall be furnished to the President, to the Secretary of the Treasury, and to the corporation concerned at the time submitted to the Congress.

Sec. 107. Whenever it is deemed by the Director of the Bureau of the Budget, with the approval of the President, to be practicable and in the public interest that any wholly owned Government corporation be treated with respect to its appropriations, expenditures, receipts, accounting, and other fiscal matters as if it were a Government agency other than a corporation, the Director shall include in connection with the budget program of such corporation in the Budget a recommendation to that effect. If the Congress approves such recommendation in connection with the budget program for any fiscal year, such corporation, with respect to subsequent fiscal years, shall be regarded as an establishment other than a corporation for the purposes of the Budget and Accounting Act, 1921, and other provisions of law relating to appropriations, expenditures, receipts, accounts, and other fiscal matters, and shall not be subject to the provisions of this Act other than this section. The corporate entity shall not be affected by this section.

TITLE II—Mixed-Ownership Government Corporations

Sec. 201. As used in this Act the term "mixed-ownership Government corporations" means (1) the Central Bank for Cooperatives and the Regional Banks for Cooperatives, (2) Federal Land Banks, (3) Federal Home Loan Banks, and (4) Federal Deposit Insurance Corporation.

Sec. 202. The financial transactions of mixed-ownership Government corporations for any period during which Government capital has been invested therein shall be audited by the General Accounting Office in accordance with the principles and procedures applicable to commercial corporate transactions and under such rules and regulations as may be prescribed by the Comptroller General of the United States. The audit shall be conducted at the place or places where the accounts of the respective corporations are normally kept. The representatives of the General Accounting Office shall have access to all books, accounts, financial records, reports, files, and all other papers, things, or property belonging to or in use by the respective corporations and necessary to facilitate the audit and they shall be afforded full facilities for verifying transactions with the balances or securities held by depositaries, fiscal agents, and custodians. The audit shall begin with the first fiscal year commencing after the enactment of this Act.

Sec. 203. A report of each such audit for each fiscal year ending on June 30 shall be made by the Comptroller General to the Congress not later than January 15, following the close of the fiscal year for which such audit is made. The report shall set forth the scope of the audit and shall include a statement (showing intercorporate relations) of assets and liabilities, capital and surplus or deficit; a statement of surplus or deficit analysis; a statement of income and expense; a statement of sources and application of funds; and such comments and information as may be deemed necessary to keep Congress informed of the operations and financial condition of, and the use of Government capital by, each such corporation, together with such recommendations with respect thereto as the Comptroller General may deem advisable, including a report of any impairment of capital or lack of sufficient capital noted in the audit and recommendations for the return of such Government capital or the payment of such dividends as, in his judgment, should be accomplished. The report shall also show specifically any program, expenditure, or other financial transaction or undertaking observed in the course of the audit, which, in the opinion of the Comptroller General, has been carried on or made without authority of law. A copy of each report shall be furnished to the President, to the Secretary of the

Treasury, and to the corporation concerned at the time submitted to the Congress.

SEC. 204. The President shall include in the annual Budget any recommendations he may wish to make as to the return of Government capital to the Treasury by any mixed-ownership corporation.

TITLE III—General Provisions

SEC. 301. (a) The expenses of auditing the financial transactions of wholly owned and mixed-ownership Government corporations as provided in sections 105 and 202 of this Act shall be borne out of appropriations to the General Accounting Office, and appropriations in such sums as may be necessary are hereby authorized: *Provided*, That each such corporation shall reimburse the General Accounting Office for the full cost of any such audit as billed therefor by the Comptroller General, and the General Accounting Office shall deposit the sums so reimbursed into the Treasury as miscellaneous receipts: *Provided further*, That in making the audits provided in said sections the Comptroller General shall, to the fullest extent deemed by him to be practicable, utilize reports of examinations of Government corporations made by a supervising administrative agency pursuant to law.

(b) For the purpose of conducting such audit the Comptroller General is authorized in his discretion to employ not more than ten persons without regard to the Classification Act of 1923, as amended, only one of whom may be compensated at a rate of as much as but not more than $10,000 per annum, and to employ by contract, without regard to section 3709 of the Revised Statutes, professional services of firms and organizations for temporary periods or for special purposes.

(c) The audit provided in sections 105 and 202 of this Act shall be in lieu of any audit of the financial transactions of any Government corporation required to be made by the General Accounting Office for the purpose of a report to the Congress or to the President under any existing law.

(d) Unless otherwise expressly provided by law, no funds of any Government corporation shall be used to pay the cost of any private audit of the financial records of the offices of such corporation, except the cost of such audits contracted for and undertaken prior to April 25, 1945.

SEC. 302. The banking or checking accounts of all wholly owned and mixed-ownership Government corporations shall be kept with the Treasurer of the United States, or, with the approval of the Secretary of the Treasury, with a Federal Reserve bank, or with a bank designated as a depositary or fiscal agent of the United States: *Provided,* That the Secretary of the Treasury may waive the requirements of this section under such conditions as he may determine: *And provided further,* That this section will not apply to the establishment and maintenance in any bank for a temporary period of banking and checking accounts not in excess of $50,000 in any one bank. The provisions of this section shall not be applicable to Federal Intermediate Credit Banks, Production Credit Corporations, the Central Bank for Cooperatives, the Regional Banks for Cooperatives, or the Federal Land Banks, except that each such corporation shall be required to report annually to the Secretary of the Treasury the names of the depositaries in which such corporation keeps a banking or checking account, and the Secretary of the Treasury may make a report in writing to the corporation, to the President, and to the Congress which he deems advisable upon receipt of any such annual report.

SEC. 303. (a) All bonds, notes, debentures, and other similar obligations which are hereafter issued by any wholly owned or mixed-ownership Government corporation and offered to the public shall be in such forms and denominations, shall have such maturities, shall bear such rates of interest, shall be subject to such terms and conditions, shall be issued in such manner and at such times and sold at such prices as have been or as may be approved by the Secretary of the Treasury.

(b) Hereafter, no wholly owned or mixed-ownership Government corporation shall sell or purchase any direct obligation of the United States or obligation guaranteed as to principal or interest, or both, for its own account and in its own right and interest, at any one time aggregating in excess of $100,000, without the approval of the Secretary of the Treasury: *Provided,* That the Secretary of the Treasury may waive the requirement of his approval with respect to any transaction or classes of transactions subject to the provisions of this subsection for such period of time and under such conditions as he may determine.

(c) The Secretary of the Treasury is hereby authorized to exercise any of the functions vested in him by this section through any officer, or employee of any Federal agency whom he may designate, with the concurrence of the head of the agency concerned, for such purpose.

(d) Any mixed-ownership Government corporation from which Government capital has been entirely withdrawn shall not be subject to the provisions of section 302 or of this section during the period such corporation remains without Government capital. The provisions of subsections (a) and (b) of this section shall not be applicable to Federal Intermediate Credit Banks, Production Credit Corporations, the Central Bank for Cooperatives, the Regional Banks for Cooperatives, or the Federal Land Banks, except that each such corporation shall be required to consult with the Secretary of the Treasury prior to taking any action of the kind covered by the provisions of subsections (a) and (b) of this section, and in the event an agreement is not reached, the Secretary of the Treasury may make a report in writing to the corporation, to the President, and to the Congress stating the grounds for his disagreement.

SEC. 304. (a) No corporation shall be created, organized, or acquired hereafter by any officer or agency of the Federal Government or by any Government corporation for the purpose of acting as an agency or instrumentality of the United States, except by Act of Congress or pursuant to an Act of Congress specifically authorizing such action.

(b) No wholly owned Government corporation created by or under the laws of any State, Territory, or possession of the United States or any political subdivision thereof, or under the laws of the District of Columbia, shall continue after June 30, 1948, as an agency or instrumentality of the United States, and no funds of, or obtained from, the United States or any agency thereof, including corporations, shall be invested in or employed by any such corporation after that date, except for purposes of liquidation. The proper corporate authority of every such corporation shall take the necessary steps to institute dissolution or liquidation proceedings on or before that date: *Provided,* That prior thereto any such corporation may be reincorporated by Act of Congress for such purposes and term of existence and with such powers, privileges, and duties as authorized by such Act, including the power to take over the assets and assume the liabilities of its respective predecessor corporation.

Approved December 6, 1945.

EXPLANATORY ILLUSTRATION OF BUDGETS FOR BUSINESS
ENTERPRISE AND REVOLVING FUNDS

Statement A
Sources and Application of Funds
[For fiscal years ending June 30, 1951, 1952, and 1953]

This is a balanced presentation of the amounts becoming available during the year, either in the form of cash or other working capital, and the way in which those amounts have been used. The statement excludes depreciation, losses on loans, and other transactions which affect neither cash nor other current assets and liabilities. It does reflect transactions which affect cash, accounts receivable, accounts payable, other accrued liabilities, inventories of supplies for administrative purposes, deferred charges and credits.

Both the "funds applied" and the "funds provided" parts of the statement are divided between "operations" and Treasury "financing." The sum of the amounts applied to operations less the amounts provided by operations equals the net expenditures, which are included within the budget expenditures for the Government as a whole.

	1951 actual	1952 estimate	1953 estimate
FUNDS APPLIED			
To operations:			
Acquisition of assets: Equipment	$ 18,238	$ 18,000	$ 18,000
Expenses:			
Purchase of materials[1]	646,616	630,000	630,000
Other expenses	877,386	966,500	966,500
Total expense	$1,524,002	$1,596,500	$1,596,500
Subtotal[2]	1,542,240	1,614,500	1,614,500
Increase in selected working capital items[3]	192,864	14,367	6,266
Total funds applied to operations	1,735,104	1,628,867	1,620,766
To financing: Increase in Treasury cash	135,633	633	------------
Total funds applied	$1,870,737	$1,629,500	$1,620,766
FUNDS PROVIDED			
By operations:			
Realization of assets: Equipment	$ 2,496	$ 3,500	$ 2,500
Income:			
Sales of goods and services	1,566,956	1,624,500	1,615,500
Rental income from quarters	1,285	1,500	1,500
Total income	$1,568,241	$1,626,000	$1,617,000
Total funds provided by operations	1,570,737	1,629,500	1,619,500
By financing:			
Appropriation	300,000	------------	------------
Decrease in Treasury cash	------------	------------	1,266
Total funds provided	$1,870,737	$1,629,500	$1,620,766

EFFECT ON BUDGETARY EXPENDITURES

Funds applied to operations	$1,735,104	$1,628,867	$1,620,766
Funds provided by operations	1,570,737	1,629,500	1,619,500
Net effect on budgetary expenditures[4]	$ 164,367	$ -633	$ 1,266
The above amounts are charged (or credited [-]) as follows:			
To budgetary authorizations[4]	300,000	------------	------------
To net receipts of the enterprise[4]	-135,633	-633	1,266

[1]Purchases for manufacture or sale are shown here, whether or not the materials are used within the year.

[2]The amounts applied to operations, other than changes in working capital, are usually broken down by object class in a supporting schedule. Where there are annual congressional limitations on administrative expenses, the object schedule is usually limited to the expenses which are under limitation.

[3]The change in selected working capital items will equal the difference between the figures on statement C for two successive years for current assets, other than Treasury cash and inventories for sale and manufacture, less current liabilities.

[4]Net effect on budgetary expenditures includes the spending of appropriations for the revolving fund as well as the spending of the fund's own receipts. A negative figure here indicates collections in excess of expenditures.

Statement B
Income and Expenses
[For fiscal years ending June 30, 1951, 1952, and 1953]

This is a statement of the income and expenses and the resulting profit or loss for the year. This statement is normally on a full accrual basis, including in the expenses sums for depreciation and provision for losses on receivables. It also indicates losses and charge-offs when they occur. In addition, gains or losses from the sale of equipment or other assets appear here.

At the bottom of this statement there is an analysis of the retained earnings or cumulative deficit, showing any additions to it during the year, any charges made against it, and the balance at the end of the year.

	1951 actual	1952 estimate	1953 estimate
Income:			
Sales of goods and services	$1,566,956	$1,624,500	$1,615,500
Rental income from quarters	1,285	1,500	1,500
Total income[1]	$1,568,241	$1,626,000	$1,617,000
Expenses:			
Cost of materials sold:			
Purchase of materials	646,616	630,000	630,000
Materials donated	3,033	2,001	3,000
Change in materials inventory	4,263	18	-----------
Cost of materials sold[2]	653,912	632,019	633,000
Other Expenses	877,386	966,500	966,500
Depreciation on equipment[3]	26,492	25,000	25,000
Total expenses	$1,557,790	$1,623,519	$1,624,500
Net income (or loss [-]) from operations	$ 10,451	$ 2,481	$ -7,500
Nonoperating income:			
Proceeds from sale of fixed assets	2,496	3,500	2,500
Net book value of assets sold	872	2,000	2,000
Gain on sale of fixed assets	$ 1,624	$ 1,500	$ 500
Net income (or loss [-]) for the year	12,075	3,981	-7,000
Retained earnings beginning of year[4]	-----------	12,075	16,056
Retained earnings end of year[4]	12,075	16,056	9,056

[1]Income (as well as expenses) is usually based on the accrual method of accounting.

[2]Cost of goods sold, rather than purchases, is considered an expense in this statement.

[3]Depreciation and other expenses not shown on statement A are indicated separately.

[4]Retained earnings here agrees with the balance sheet. It represents cumulative profits kept in the business, whether in the form of cash, inventories, receivables, or fixed assets.

Statement C
Financial Condition
[As of June 30, 1951, 1952, and 1953]

This is a balance sheet of assets, liabilities, and investment of the Government at the close of the fiscal year. Like the other statements, it is normally on an accrual basis.

The section for the Government's financial interest is broken down to indicate the amount which has been invested by the Government on which the fund pays interest (if any), the amount invested on which the fund does not pay interest, and the retained earnings or deficit.

	1951 actual	1952 estimate	1953 estimate
ASSETS			
Current assets:			
Cash with U. S. Treasury[1]	$ 135,633	$ 136,266	$ 135,000
Accounts receivable	345,044	340,000	340,000
Inventory of supplies and materials	95,019	95,001	95,001
Total current assets	$ 575,696	$ 571,267	$ 570,001
Fixed assets:			
Equipment	291,451	295,451	299,451
Less portion charged off as depreciation	101,648	114,648	127,648
Total fixed assets	$ 189,803	$ 180,803	$ 171,803
Total assets	$ 765,499	$ 752,070	$ 741,804
LIABILITIES			
Current liabilities:			
Accounts payable	124,073	110,000	104,734
Accrued expenses	126,338	121,000	120,000
Total liabilities[2]	$ 250,411	$ 231,000	$ 224,734
INVESTMENT OF U. S. GOVERNMENT			
Principal of fund;			
Appropriation	300,000	300,000	300,000
Donated assets, net	203,013	205,014	208,014
Total principal of fund	503,013	505,014	508,014
Retained earnings	12,075	16,056	9,056
Total investment of U. S. Government[3]	$ 515,088	$ 521,070	$ 517,070
Total liabilities and investment of U. S. Government	$ 765,499	$ 752,070	$ 741,804

[1]Cash with United States Treasury is the sum that the fund has on deposit with the Treasury. It excludes any balances of appropriations (or other authorizations) which have not yet been paid into the business enterprise or revolving fund.

[2]Liabilities normally means what is owed for goods and services which have been received. The remainder excludes obligations outstanding for items on order of: $23,410 as of June 30, 1951, $23,000 as of June 30, 1952, and $23,000 as of June 30, 1953.

[3]The investment of the United States Government indicates the Government's interest as owner, plus the Government's interest as creditor in the form of notes payable to the Treasury where a Government corporation has authorization to borrow on such notes.